Proclaiming the Baptist Vision

Religious Liberty

Other volumes in the series include:

Volume 1, *Proclaiming the Baptist Vision*
  The Priesthood of All Believers

Volume 2, *Proclaiming the Baptist Vision*
  The Bible

Volume 3, *Proclaiming the Baptist Vision*
  The Church

Volume 5, *Proclaiming the Baptist Vision*
  Baptism and the Lord's Supper

Proclaiming the Baptist Vision

Religious Liberty

Walter B. Shurden
Editor

SMYTH & HELWYS
PUBLISHING, INC.
MACON, GEORGIA

ISBN 1-57312-169-X

Proclaiming the Baptist Vision
Religious Liberty

Walter B. Shurden, editor

Copyright 1997
Smyth & Helwys Publishing, Inc.®
6316 Peake Road
Macon, Georgia 31210-3960
1-800-568-1248

All rights reserved.
Printed in the United States of America.

The paper used in this publication meets the minimum requirements of American Standard for Information Sciences—Permanence of Paper for Printed Library Materials, ANSI Z39.48–1984.

Library of Congress Cataloging-in-Publication Data

Religious liberty / Walter B. Shurden, editor.
   168 + vi pages 6 x 9" (15 x 23 cm.)
   — (Proclaiming the Baptist Vision; v.4)
Includes bibliographical references.
ISBN 1-57312-169-X (alk. paper)
    1. Freedom of religion—United States—Sermons.
    2. Baptists—Sermons. 3. Sermons, American.
    I. Shurden, Walter B.
    II. Series.
BV741.R436 1997
261.7'2'088261—dc21   97-14477
                                                CIP

Contents

Introduction 1
    Walter B. Shurden

I. Baptist History and Religious Liberty

1. How We Got That Way: Baptists on Religious Liberty
   and Separation of Church and State 13
   Walter B. Shurden

II. Baptist Foundations and Religious Liberty

2. The Baptist Vision of Religious Liberty 31
   James M. Dunn

3. Religious Liberty: Gift and Opportunity 39
   William H. Brackney

4. Freedom Is a State of Mind 45
   Carolyn DeArmond Blevins

5. The Christian and the State 53
   Roger Hayden

III. Baptist Treasures on Religious Liberty

6. Baptists and Religious Liberty 61
   George W. Truett

7. The Baptist Conception of Religious Liberty 85
   E. Y. Mullins

8. The American Baptist Bill of Rights 95

IV. Baptists and Current Issues of Religious Liberty

9. Religious Liberty: A Continuing Struggle 101
   Brent Walker

10. Praying in Public 109
    Michael Bledsoe

11. The Kind of Prayer That Honors God and That God Honors . 119
    Stan Hastey

12. Civil Religion and Religious Liberty 127
    Derek H. Davis

13. Freedom Talk: Conversations of Jesus with Baptists 135
    J. Alfred Smith, Sr.

V. Baptist Personalities and Religious Liberty

14. The Mystery of Iniquity: The Helwys Tradition 143
    Rosalie Beck

15. A Visit From John Clarke 151
    Thomas R. McKibbens, Jr.

16. The Love of God and the Worth of Immortal Souls:
    A Monologue Sermon on John Leland 157
    R. Quinn Pugh

Biographical Notes 167

Introduction

by Walter B. Shurden

Why a book of sermons at the end of the twentieth century on Baptists and religious liberty? For several reasons.

One, the first words of the first amendment to the Constitution of the United States state: "Congress shall make no law respecting an establishment of religion, or prohibiting the free exercise thereof." For all their apparent clarity, I believe those words constitute some of the most crucial, complicated, and conflictual words facing American life in the closing days of the twentieth century and the beginning of the twenty-first century.

Religious liberty and the knotty topic of how religion and government relate consume a significant portion of the legislative and judicial processes in America today. Seldom a day passes that a daily newspaper does not carry an article related to some aspect of the topic. Much of the social conflict tearing at the fabric of this republic stems from such issues as prayer in public schools, the posting of the Ten Commandments, federal aid for parochial education, and efforts to amend the first amendment. That fact notwithstanding, it is exceedingly difficult to convince many contemporary Americans that first amendment issues are critical issues, another reason, I suppose, for a book on the subject.

Two, I believe that many conservative American Christians are misled by people who, understandably concerned about the current moral state of America, appear to want to transform this republic into a Christian state. The mind set that views America's past as "a Christian nation" muddles up the clarity of the first amendment, misinterprets America's history and constitution, disregards fundamental issues of religious liberty, and, maybe most importantly, diminishes the meaning of "Christian." It is, however, a dangerous and insidious mind set with a powerful popular appeal.

An important note, however, is that certainly not all conservative Christians in America agree with the effort of correcting present moral ills by interpreting America's past in Christian categories. Indeed, three of the most respected evangelical, conservative Christian historians in America took it upon themselves to confront and correct this interpretation. These three are Mark Noll, Nathan Hatch, and George Marsden. Together they wrote an extremely important book entitled *The Search For Christian America*,[1] a work that deserves wide circulation in the churches of this country.

The single-most important thing about the book is its thesis. Noll, Hatch, and Marsden argue that the popular notion that America has been, ever was, or is now a Christian nation is a serious distortion of historical reality. Moreover, that distortion, they insist, is not only historically skewed, it is biblically and theologically deficient and practically hurtful to contemporary Christians as they try to apply their faith to the burning issues of society.

Why raise the issue of America as a Christian nation when addressing the topic of religious liberty? Because the two issues inevitably mesh. Those who insist on the "Christian" character of this country often end up debunking the separation of church and state, reinterpreting the first amendment to the U.S. Constitution, and playing fast and loose with the precious commodity of religious liberty.

A third reason for a book of sermons on Baptists and religious liberty is to restate at the end of the twentieth century the Baptist vision of religious liberty during a time when, ironically, many Baptists have simply forgotten their denominational heritage on this issue. Historically, church-state relationships have been difficult, even tortuous. One may even find within the pages of the New Testament diverse interpretations of church-state relations. Jesus recognized both the limitations and legitimacy of the state, according to Matthew 22:15-22. During a time when Christians were not in danger from the state, Paul, in Romans 13:1-7, accented the legitimacy of the state. During a time of persecution, however, the writer of Revelation 13 advocated resistance to the state to the point of martyrdom.

No one approach accommodates all circumstances of history. Baptist Christians, among others, have acknowledged the diversity of biblical teaching on the relation of church and state. Often appreciative of the blessings of civil government, Baptists have been "Romans 13 People." Occasionally opposing the state with their very lives, they have been "Revelation 13 People." Most of the time, however, they have been "Matthew 22 People," legitimizing but limiting the state. In their persistent call for religious freedom and separation of church and state, however, Baptists have been consistent, until recent days.

Having bought into the point of view described above that America should be viewed as a Christian nation, many contemporary Baptists, said distinguished Baptist church historian William R. Estep, "appear to be confused, with no clear notion of who they are amidst the pied pipers of the New Right."[2] Estep's book ought to be required reading for Baptists, indeed, for all people, religious or irreligious, who care deeply about the First Amendment. This respected Baptist scholar carefully documents the historical Baptist position on religious liberty and separation of church and state. He also identifies those Baptists who have abandoned that position, indicating why they have done so. He maintains that Baptists have emerged in the closing decades of the twentieth century who are opposed to separation of church and state, and that this position represents a "radical break" with the traditional Baptist vision. Some present-day Baptists, says Estep, suffer from an "identity crisis."[3]

A final reason for this book on Baptists and religious liberty is that it is the fourth in a series of five books designed to present historic Baptist convictions in substantive sermonic form by some of Baptists' best preachers. The first volume, published in 1993, highlighted the Baptist emphasis on the priesthood of all believers, while the second volume, published in 1994, centered on the Bible. The third volume described the Baptist vision of the church. This present volume, focusing on religious liberty, will be followed by a final volume in 1998, concentrating on the Baptist view of the ordinances of baptism and the Lord's Supper.

I have deviated here slightly from the three previously published books in this series by placing the historical and theological essay at the beginning rather than at the conclusion of the sermons. In this particular volume, the essay made a better introduction than conclusion to the sermons. Following the introductory historical essay, a group of four sermons address the general subject of "Baptist Foundations and Religious Liberty." James Dunn, the leading Baptist voice in America on behalf of religious liberty of our time, has the lead sermon in this volume and argues that religious liberty is rooted in nothing less than the creative act of God. God's stamp upon human beings made us responsible, therefore free. A human being made in the image of God presupposes freedom. We are "choosers." Dunn calls that aspect of our existence "Soul Freedom," and it is, in his judgment, the first phase of religious liberty. From soul freedom, Dunn says, comes "religious liberty," and he underscores that this is religious liberty FOR ALL. And from the principle of religious liberty comes its political corollary: separation of church and state. For Dunn, therefore, a comprehensive view of religious liberty contains three parts. "Soul Freedom" is the individual component; "religious liberty" is the social component; "separation of church and state" is the political component.

Regarding the last, the separation of church and state, Dunn, who knows the intricacies of church-state separation as well as anyone, acknowledges that "Separation is not neat. It's messy, difficult, inconsistent, and it always has been." Despite the difficulties, Dunn insists that we must have some "wall of separation," even if it is nothing more than "a strand of barbed wire."

William H. Brackney, principal of McMaster Divinity College in Hamilton, Ontario, Canada, and a leading authority on the Baptist heritage, calls us in his sermon to embrace religious liberty as both "a gift and an opportunity." He insists in his sermon, as he does elsewhere in his writings, that at the core of the Baptist understanding of freedom is the "voluntary principle."[4] After demonstrating the scriptural bases of the voluntary principle, Brackney applies the principle to Baptist benevolence, Baptist ecumenism, and Baptist missions.

Is religious freedom a matter of rules and law and statutes? In her sermon Carolyn DeArmond Blevins says that freedom "is a state of mind." Demonstrating that this state of mind is rooted in the very action of God and the whole of biblical history, Blevins identifies three attitudes basic to the life of religious liberty. Those attitudes are trust, respect, and fairness.

Says Blevins,

> Freedom of religion is not new; it did not originate in America. Religious freedom is biblical; it came with the divine act of creation. God gave freedom of religion to the created ones. God never forced faith on anyone!

Blevins echoes and reaffirms Dunn and Brackney that religious freedom came "with the divine act of creation."

In his sermon, Roger Hayden, British Baptist minister, addresses the topic of "The Christian and the State." Arguing that the early church recognized that the power of the state *could* be the vehicle of God's rule for good, Hayden asserts, "It is the difficulty of discovering whether the powers that be *are* ordained of God, which is one of the most critical decisions for Christians today."

Living in a nation without a history of church-state separation, Hayden asks the question troubling many Americans today, "What is the role of the Church in a Nation?" Without calling for a theocracy, Hayden answers by saying that the church must pursue the principles embodied within the Kingdom of God. He identifies four such principles. First, the church should seek an open society where there is total separation of church and state. Second, Hayden calls the church to seek a society that recognizes the reality of sin and therefore works for power-sharing. Third, the church must seek a society that confronts collective sins, "a society that is concerned with justice *and* righteousness, a society that faces the politics of caring for humankind not only locally, but nationally and internationally." Fourth, Hayden believes that the church should work for a society that knows "the proper place of law" by tempering justice with mercy.

While the first set of sermons all come from contemporary Baptists—Dunn, Brackney, Blevins, and Hayden—the second group of documents emanate from the Baptist past and constitute "Baptist Treasures on Religious Liberty." Two of these documents are sermons delivered by George W. Truett and E. Y. Mullins, both of whom had enormous influence in the first quarter of the twentieth century on Baptists around the world. The last document is not a sermon, but it is included because of its adoption by the three largest Baptist groups in America in 1939.

The sermon by George W. Truett, delivered on the steps of the national Capitol in 1920, is one of the most often quoted Baptist statements on religious liberty of the twentieth century. Heretofore not readily accessible, it is reprinted here to make it available. Its reprinting here, however, is because of its historical value, and so it can serve as a comparison to contemporary Baptist understandings of religious freedom. Truett served as pastor of the First Baptist Church in Dallas, Texas, for forty-seven years and as president of the Southern Baptist Convention and the Baptist World Alliance. He both shaped and reflected the Baptist vision during his era.

One must carefully keep in mind "his era" while reading the sermon. The denominational huffiness and the Catholic-Protestant animosities were more acute in the 1920s than during our time. While Truett's sermon contains an overwhelmingly pro-Baptist sound (too much so for those of us who are ecumenical Baptists), you will also find the note of genuine appreciation for other religious traditions. Truett doubtless failed to give adequate credit for the contributions of other religious groups in the struggle for religious liberty, yet he was on solid ground in highlighting the Baptist contribution.

Truett's sermon may also sound harshly anti-Catholic to our ears almost eighty years later. A careful reading, however, will see that while Truett carefully delineated the differences between Baptists and Catholics, he also warmly expressed an interest in religious liberty for Catholics as well as Baptists. Truett demonstrates that one can hold convictions firmly while, at the same time, granting to others the same liberties one desires for oneself.

In addition to showing how many of the Baptist distinctives relate to the theme of religious liberty, Truett clearly delineated between the Baptist understanding of religious liberty and religious toleration. He said,

> There is a wide difference between toleration and liberty. Toleration implies that somebody falsely claims the right to tolerate. Toleration is a concession, while liberty is a right. Toleration is a matter of expediency, while liberty is a matter of principle. Toleration is a gift from man, while liberty is a gift from God.

E. Y. Mullins, for twenty-nine years the president of The Southern Baptist Theological Seminary in Louisville, Kentucky, also, as did Truett, served as president of both the Southern Baptist Convention and the Baptist World Alliance. At the Baptist World Alliance meeting in Stockholm in 1923, Mullins preached a sermon titled "The Baptist Conception of Religious Liberty." It is one of the most important addresses ever presented at a meeting of the BWA, and maybe one of the most important Baptist sermons on religious liberty ever preached. Mullins delivered his sermon amidst the concerns of a postwar world, especially political and ecclesiastical persecution in Europe.

As with the sermon by Truett, the reader should keep in mind the date of the sermon—1923. Preached almost a half century before Vatican II, before vast and significant changes in the Roman Catholic Church, and before major alterations in Protestant-Catholic relations, the sermon carries the Protestant-Catholic animosities of Mullins's time. Were Mullins preaching today, he doubtless would alter some of the harshness of his rhetoric in the latter part of the sermon. I am also confident that, were he living today, he would also have utilized more gender-free language, and I have adapted his sermon in this regard.

Mullins's sermon is not only a sermon on religious liberty; it is a distillation of historic Baptist distinctives. It deserves wide circulation. Baptist preachers today would do well to use much of Mullins's and Truett's sermons as models for preaching the theme of religious liberty.

After describing the bases of religious liberty, Mullins says that religious liberty excludes "certain things." Those certain things that religious liberty excludes are: state authority in religion, the principle of toleration in religion, the right of the state to impose taxes for the support of one form of religion, the imposition of religious creeds, centralized ecclesiastical government, priestly mediators and sacramental powers of salvation, and infant baptism.

Religious liberty implies "certain things" as well. These are: the right of direct access to God, the right of free utterance and propagation of truth; the right of equal privileges in the church; the right of free association and organization for religious purposes; the right of people to demand of government protection in the free exercise of their religion.

Mullins spoke finally about the "duties" of religious liberty. He enumerated these duties as the following: the duty to search for and discover truth, the duty to sacrifice for truth, the duty to protect against religious persecution, the duty of loyalty to the state, and the supreme duty of loyalty to Jesus Christ.

The third document included in the section on "Baptist Treasures on Religious Liberty," is, as stated above, nonsermonic in character. It was adopted unanimously in 1939 by The National Baptist Convention (20 September 1939), The Northern Baptist Convention (21 June 1939), and The Southern Baptist Convention (20 May 1939). As such, the document is important because it represents the point of view of the three largest Baptist denominations in the United States at that time. The version printed in this book is copied from the 1939 SBC *Annual*, pages 114-16.

Sounding very contemporary, the 1939 document begins with the assertion that "no issue in modern life is more urgent or more complicated than the relation of organized religion to organized society." After rehearsing the four theories of church-state relations and the role of Baptists in establishing religious liberty, the document enumerates "the principles that animate the activities of the Baptists."

These Baptists were constrained to declare their position on religious liberty in 1939 because, as they said, and again sounding very contemporary,

> every session of the Congress considers legislation that raises the question as to the relation of the Federal Government to the institutions and agencies of religion, and . . . many tendencies have appeared that involve the freedom of religion and conscience.

Closing with a spirited defense of religious freedom, the document said:

> Believing religious liberty to be not only an inalienable human right, but indispensable to human welfare, Baptists must exercise themselves to the utmost in the maintenance of absolute religious liberty for their Jewish neighbors, their Catholic neighbors, their Protestant neighbors, and for everybody else. Profoundly convinced that any deprivation of this right is a wrong to be challenged, Baptists condemn every form of compulsion in religion or restraint of the free consideration of the claims of religion.

Following the collection of "Baptist Treasures on Religious Liberty," you will find five sermons from contemporary Baptists addressing the general theme of "Baptists and Current Issues of Religious Liberty." The first of these sermons is by Brent Walker, legal counsel for the Baptist Joint Committee in Washington, and one of the most knowledgeable Baptists today regarding church-state issues. Walker thinks it is not enough for Baptists to rest on their laurels regarding past work in advocating religious liberty; he wants us to be aware of the current threats to religious freedom, especially in America.

Walker documents that, among all people, some contemporary Baptists in America have lost their way on the issue of religious liberty and separation of church and state. Says Walker,

> A quick look at four pressing church–state issues of the final decade of the 20th century confirm that some Baptists have forgotten our heritage, and that we need to redouble our efforts to turn our heritage into a legacy.

The "four pressing church-state issues" Walker identifies are: (1) the Religious Freedom Restoration Act of 1993, (2) federal and state aid to parochial schools, (3) The New Welfare Bill and state monies to church ministries, and (4) the effort to amend the religion clause in the Bill of Rights.

Following Walker's sermon, pastor Michael Bledsoe and denominational executive Stan Hastey each present sermons on the issue of prayer in public schools. Bledsoe and Hastey even use the same scripture text in approaching their subject. Several differences exist between the two sermons, however. For one thing, Bledsoe's sermon is congregationally focused at a specific moment in history whereas Hastey's is more generic in nature. Both are helpful models for understanding the issue.

Bledsoe preached his sermon in the pulpit of the church where he is pastor. Allusions to the church occur near the end of the sermon and are instructive for pastors in applying the issue to the local setting. Bledsoe believes that "the historic Baptist commitment to liberty is a commitment to telling the truth, and it is not coincidental that such truth-telling took its turn pointing into the face of an intrusive State." Among other things, Bledsoe tells us why so much concern abounds in America today regarding prayer in public schools. Quoting James Dunn, who was quoting Pitirim Sorokin, Bledsoe says that we are living in the "Day of Dead Flowers." By that he means we live in a culture void of the roots of religious experience and commitment. Clearly opposed to a constitutional amendment "to put *public praying* back in public schools," Bledsoe says,

> Historically Baptists have opposed such an amendment. Has the time come to change that position? I will argue that it has not and that in these dangerous times and for the sake of religious liberty, it is especially important that we resist this temptation.

Bledsoe offers no simplistic approach, though his point of view is crystal clear. Affirming the need of prayer for our parched souls and the need for transmitting values to our children, he nonetheless implores Baptists to try another way than that of a constitutional amendment.

Stan Hastey has emerged in the last several years as one of the sanest and most insightful voices regarding the Baptist heritage. Because of his long tenure on the staff of the Baptist Joint Committee in Washington

DC, and his more recent leadership of The Alliance of Baptists, Stan Hastey has thought long and hard about the issue of prayer in public schools. As a traditional Baptist committed to the separation of church and state, he comes down on both feet opposed to the practice of prayer in public schools. Some will be surprised that his major reason for doing so, however, is theological, although he can argue the constitutional issues as well as anyone. Hastey contends that "the prayer that is worth anything at all is the kind of prayer that honors God and that God honors."

Derek H. Davis, director of the J. M. Dawson Institute on Church and State at Baylor University, presents an insightful sermon that seeks to restore the positive meaning of "Civil Religion" while at the same time not compromising Baptists' understanding of church and state. Openly acknowledging that "civil religion" has a shadow side to it—exalting nationalism above the Kingdom of God—Davis believes that there is a religious character to the body politic that Baptists can plug into and that supports the Baptist drive for religious liberty.

J. Alfred Smith, Sr., one of the best contemporary Baptist preachers, puts a prophetic spin on his sermon on freedom. Rather than addressing specifically the issue of religious freedom, he targets the contemporary cultural captivity of Baptists of North America. With his "freedom talk" with major Baptist groups in America, Smith raises questions about how much Baptists believe in genuine liberty today—for themselves. With a heritage advocating religious liberty, are Baptists themselves in bondage? Smith suggests it may be so.

The final three sermons in this volume focus on important Baptist personalities who fought for religious liberty, and the sermons thereby offer a different way of presenting the subject. Rosalie Beck, professor of religion at Baylor University in Waco, Texas, roots her sermon in the lives and ministries of Thomas and Joan Helwys, early founders of the Baptist tradition in England. Thomas McKibbens, Jr., and Quinn Pugh each present a dramatic monologue sermon based on the lives of John Clarke and John Leland respectively. With each of these three sermons one learns specific Baptist stories and the relevance of those stories for Baptist life today. What Beck, McKibbens, and Pugh have done with the subjects of their sermons could be just as easily done with a number of Baptist personalities.

As indicated in the three previously published volumes in this series, my goal in *Proclaiming the Baptist Vision* is to provide both clergy and laity easy access to understanding the historic Baptist distinctives. One may wonder why, in an era that many label as "post-denominational," one would bother with denominational distinctives at all. Rest assured that it is not because the authors of these sermons or I believe that Baptists have a monopoly on God. That is not the case at all. I do live with the conviction, however, that one can be genuinely committed to the broader ecumenical church without ignoring or disregarding the particular religious tradition that has shaped one's life. Moreover, I happen to believe that the Baptist tradition of Christianity and its historic emphases are more important at this present time than at any other time during the twentieth century.

I decided to use sermons as the method of presenting Baptist distinctives for a couple of reasons. First, good, substantive sermons represent a literary form attractive to the laity. Second, I utilized the sermon as the form for presenting these distinctives because I wanted to provide Baptist preachers with some models and materials for helping them with their pulpit ministry. If communicating the Baptist tradition has any merit at all, it should be done on Sunday morning at 11:00 A.M., when most of our people are present for worship. We cannot relegate the teaching of Christian history or denominational emphases to occasional seminars where only the already-convinced attend. If a subject is genuinely important for the life of the church, then surely that subject must contend for time at the one hour when most people are present. Religious freedom, the historic Baptist affirmation of freedom OF religion, freedom FOR religion, and freedom FROM religion, is such a topic. It deserves a place in the pulpit of America, especially a place in the pulpits of Baptists in America.

Notes

[1] Mark Noll, Nathan O. Hatch, and George M. Marsden, *The Search for Christian America* (Colorado Springs CO: Helmers and Howard, Publishers, Inc., 1989). The address for securing a copy of the book is Helmers and Howard Publishers, P.O. Box 7407, Colorado Springs, Colorado, 80933.

[2] William R. Estep, *Revolution Within the Revolution: The First Amendment in Historical Context, 1612–1789* (Grand Rapids MI: William B. Eerdmans Publishing Company, 1990) 9.

[3] Ibid.

[4] See especially William H. Brackney, "Voluntarism Is a Flagship of the Baptist Tradition," in Charles W. Deweese, ed., *Defining Baptist Convictions* (Franklin TN: Providence House Publishers, 1996)86-94.

How We Got That Way
Baptists on Religious Liberty and Separation of Church and State

Walter B. Shurden

[*This paper was presented at the sixtieth-anniversary celebration of the Baptist Joint Committee in Washington DC on 8 October 1996. It is slightly revised here for publication in this volume.*]

In the United States one can count 28,921,564 individual Baptists in 122,811 local churches in 63 different denominational bodies.[1] Worldwide one can identify 37,334,191 Baptists in 157,240 local Baptist churches.[2] Those are impressive statistics of no small measure. So why then does that idiosyncratic Baptist farmer preacher, Will Campbell, say in several of his books that not many Baptists exist any longer? What Campbell means, I gather, is that not many Baptists continue to act out of the muscular Baptist tradition of freedom, including religious liberty and separation of church and state.

How is it in your part of the country? Are Baptists widely and popularly recognized today as the "stout champions of freedom"? Or is the popular image of Baptists in your part of the world by non-Baptists what it is in mine? And that is that we are narrow, provincial, even reactionary Christians, not freedom-loving freedom-fighters. Baptists in many places today are not seen as those who keep a sickle in their hands to root out the weeds of oppression and totalitarianism in the garden of life.

Walker Percy, the psychiatrist turned novelist, was, for my money, one of the most prophetic and perceptive readers of American life in the last half of the nineteenth century. Here is what Percy said about the Baptists he knew in the deep South. He said they are a group of evangelistically repulsive anti-Catholics who are political opportunists advocating scientific creationism in the public school system.³

Surely one must not swallow uncritically Walker Percy's assessment. I do not. But I concede that he was in fact describing what many **assume** the Baptist identity to be today. Baptists are simply not perceived as freedom-lovers and freedom-givers and freedom-protectors by many persons in America today. If that is the case, and I think to a great degree it is, it is sad, sad, sad.

It means that Baptists have come a long, long way from home, from their humble beginnings and struggling origins. Most of us when we think of Baptists and freedom in the last half of the twentieth century could probably point to only three movements: (1) African-American Baptists and the struggle for civil rights in America, (2) the Baptist World Alliance and its involvement in religious liberty and human rights issues around the globe, and (3) The Baptist Joint Committee in Washington DC and its pit-bulldog defense of religious freedom and separation of church and state in the United States.

We can thank God for all three because, each in its own way, has rung sharply and loudly the note of freedom, a note that has become fainter and fainter for some Baptists in the last half of this century. Today many Baptists know the words of freedom, but they have forgotten the music. But both the music and the words in the Baptist heritage speak words and make melodies of no uncertain sound. Both the lyrics and the tunes in the Baptist past speak harmoniously and unambiguously of absolute religious liberty based upon principle, not expediency. And they speak of the political derivative of religious liberty, the separation of church and state.

How did we Baptists get to these ideas of absolute religious liberty and separation of church and state? There is no doubt that we did. Even some of our fiercest historical opponents affirm this. So how did Baptists get beyond "establishmentarianism," which was so much a part of the concept of Christendom in Europe and England and New England and in most of the American colonies?

And how did Baptists get beyond mere "tolerationism"? Tolerationism, while a gigantic step beyond establishmentarianism, never discovered the spacious land of freedom of conscience. And how did Baptists get beyond "accommodationism"? Accommodationism—the seductive idea that all Christian denominations would share equally in the bounty of the state—how did Baptists get beyond that one?

In some instances, as Baptist history will document, we sputtered at times in getting beyond accommodationism, but in the end our forebears recognized its inadequacies and inequities and "leveler" heads prevailed. How did Baptists get to these heady ideas of religious freedom for absolutely everybody and separation of church and state for both the good of the church and the good of the state? As I said, there is no question that Baptists got there. How did they?

I will suggest that Baptists finally got that way because of three factors. First, Baptists got that way because they were **birthed in adversity**. Second, Baptists got that way because **their peculiar Christian convictions and common-sense encouraged theological diversity**. Third, Baptists got that way on religious liberty and separation of church and state because, birthed in adversity and with Christian convictions encouraging theological diversity, **they inevitably sealed their convictions by engaging in political activity**. They got that way because of their **birthing**, their **believing**, and their way of **being** in the world.

Baptists: Birthed in Historical Adversity

Baptists came from the womb of the seventeenth-century English Reformation and landed immediately in hostile territory. Almost twenty-five years ago I published a little book entitled *Not A Silent People: Controversies That Have Shaped Southern Baptists*.[4] Some may recall that I entitled the very first chapter "Here Come the Battling Baptists." After twenty-five years I remain convinced of the appropriateness of the title of the first chapter to describe the emergence of Baptists as a distinct denomination.

Baptists emerged as a specific body in the midst of a crippling adversity. They came battling! If you ever write a historical essay on early Baptist life in either England or the American Colonies, a good place to begin your research is in the records of court proceedings, search warrants, and prison records. While that story of repression and oppression may be over-dramatized, and even skewed in a comprehensive retelling of the Baptist story, it is nonetheless a fact that Baptists bled in their earliest years of the seventeenth century, and they remained handcuffed in much of the eighteenth century. They bled from the whip of religious oppression, and they were constricted by the arms of both church and state and of the two acting in concert.

The historical context is crucial. Queen Elizabeth reigned in England from 1558–1603, the last half of the sixteenth century, and she tried valiantly to settle the problem of an emerging religious pluralism in England. The Queen attempted to build a tent big enough to accommodate a passionate, powerful, and proliferating pluralism. She failed. The old dream of the Medieval Synthesis with all of life united around a single ruler and a single expression of religion was slowly crumbling in the dust of blazing individual freedoms. In the end, the so-called Elizabethan Settlement settled nothing.

When Elizabeth died in 1603, James I, formerly James VI of Scotland, came to the throne, stirring hope in the hearts of Puritans and more radical dissenters. After all James was coming from The Church of Scotland. But Puritans and nonconformists hoped in vain. James' immediate and persistent remedy for the knotty problem of religious fragmentation in England was simple: forced uniformity!

James I and Charles I, who succeeded James and who reigned till 1649, both reacted with horror to the idea of liberty of conscience. Rather, James and Charles affirmed the divine right of kings and the divine right of bishops as one and the same. It was a scrambled-eggs society. Church and State came on the same plate and all mixed together. Baptists, virtual babies on the religious scene, tried to unscramble the political-ecclesiastical eggs, maintaining, among other things, that the state has no say-so over the soul of a person.

During James' reign from 1603–1625, the Separatists, from whom the Baptists would themselves eventually separate, multiplied. The Separatists had no reason to be surprised, however, when the King's fist came down hard on them. Less than a year after coming to the throne, James I called the Hampton Court Conference in January 1604 to deal with the petitions made by the Puritans, a people not nearly so liberal as the Separatists, for reform in the church. When the Puritans demanded modification of the episcopacy, James declared, "No bishop, no king." And then reacting to the slightest tinge of religious liberty, James said in kingly fear and sarcasm:

> Jack and Tom and Will and Dick shall meete, and at their pleasure censure me and my Councell and all our proceedings. Then Will shall stand up and say it must be thus; then Dick shall reply and say, nay, narry, but we shall have it thus[5]

James I, like so many of his age, caricatured religious pluralism because he simply could not imagine a society built on the freedom to choose one's faith. And so that there could be no mistake of the King's point of view, James declared of the Puritans at Hampton, "I shall make them conforme themselves, or I wil harrie them out of the land, or else doe worse."

It was during James' reign that the little group at Gainsborough, led by John Smyth and Thomas Helwys, pioneers of the Baptist movement, left their homeland of England in 1608 to find religious refuge in Holland.

And it was during Charles' reign that folks swarmed to New England to escape the merciless hand of Archbishop William Laud. Laud, who became Archbishop of Canterbury in 1633, and Charles I, the monarch who favored him so, would in the end both feel the sting of political and religious persecution in their own executions.

And it was during both reigns of James and Charles that Baptists peppered both royalty and religion with some of the first and most forceful tracts ever written on religious liberty.

John Smyth's 1612 "Propositions and Conclusions" was, according to William Lumpkin, "perhaps the first confession of faith of modern times to demand freedom of conscience and separation of church and state"[6] Said Smyth,

> The magistrate is not by virtue of his office to meddle with religion, or matters of conscience, to force or compel men to this or that form of religion, or doctrine: but to leave Christian religion free, to every man's conscience . . . for Christ only is the king, and lawgiver of the church and conscience (James 4:12).[7]

Thomas Helwys, upon returning to England with a remnant of Smyth's group, released in 1612 his document entitled *A Short Declaration of the Mistery of Iniquity*. He was rewarded with a prison sentence, but not before this pioneer Baptist freely professed of the Roman Catholics of England that

> our lord the King hath no more power over their consciences then ours, and that is none at all: for our Lord the King is but an earthly King, and if the Kings people be obedient & true subjects, obeying all humane lawes made by the King, our lord the King, can require no more. For mens religion to God, is betwixt God and themselves; the King shall not

answer for it; neither may the King be judg betwene God and man. Let them be heretikes, Turks, Jewes or whatsoever, it apperteynes not to the earthly power to punish them in the least measure.[8]

First, Smyth; second, Helwys; and then Leonard Busher. Busher wrote *Religion's Peace: A Plea for Liberty of Conscience*, which Leon McBeth called "the first Baptist treatise devoted exclusively to religious liberty."[9] Published in 1614, Busher asserted that "as kings and bishops cannot command the wind, so they cannot command faith." He continued, writing the following in capital letters: "IT IS NOT ONLY UNMERCIFUL, BUT UNNATURAL AND ABOMINABLE; YEA, MONSTROUS FOR ONE CHRISTIAN TO VEX AND DESTROY ANOTHER FOR DIFFERENCE AND QUESTIONS OF RELIGION."[10]

Following Busher, John Murton in *Persecution for Religion Judg'd and Condemn'd* (1615, 1620, 1662) confessed he was compelled to write because of "how heinous it is in the sight of the Lord to force men and women by cruel persecution, to bring their bodies to a worship whereunto they cannot bring their spirits."[11] Starkly, he wrote, "that no man ought to be persecuted of his religion, be it true or false."[12]

It is important to pause and remember that Baptists in the seventeenth century confronted religious restrictionism from both the courthouse and the churchhouse, from both the monarchs of England and the bishops of the Church of England. It did not end there, however. Neither the Puritans, the Presbyterians, nor the Separatists in England advocated complete soul liberty. And things were no better in New England. There Obadiah Holmes was publicly whipped on the streets of Boston. And as a result, John Clarke, pastor of the First Baptist Church in Newport, Rhode Island, presented a document to Old England with the ominous title of "Ill Newes From New England."

There, in the New World, Isaac Backus had to write as late as 1773 a pleading work entitled "An Appeal to the Public for Religious Liberty." Two decades later John Leland (1791) wrote a pamphlet, "The Rights of Conscience Inalienable," saying that "Government has no more to do with the religious opinions of men, than it has with the principles of mathematics." Leland continued,

> Let every man speak freely without fear, maintain the principles that he believes, worship according to his own faith, either one God, three Gods, no God, or twenty Gods; and let government protect him in so doing.[13]

So born in the midst of great pain with freedom denied, Baptists, a minority people, grounded their affirmation for religious freedom to some degree in their own historical experience of deprivation. There is nothing quite so strong as the testimony of the oppressed, unless it is the testimony of the oppressed that has gone public so that all can see and hear. You will remember that Martin Luther King, Jr., was criticized because, as some said, "He was simply trying to attract the media." King responded that such was precisely what he was trying to do. He sought to attract a crowd to expose to the nation and the world the denial of basic human rights. Helwys, Busher, Murton, Clarke, Williams, Backus, and Leland penned their fiery tracts and pamphlets for precisely the same reason. As the Civil Rights Movement of the 1960s was born from freedoms denied, just so the Religious Rights Movement of the seventeenth and eighteenth centuries. Baptists "got that way" on religious liberty and separation of church and state because they were born in adversity.

Baptists: Christian Convictions That Encouraged Diversity

Second, Baptists got that way on these issues because their Baptist interpretation of the Christian faith and human life encouraged theological diversity. Let us be sure of what I am saying. To say that their convictions encouraged diversity does not suggest in the least that Baptists had no firm certainties regarding cardinal Christian truths, nor is it to say that their opinions were flabby with an "anything goes" approach to the Bible and theology. They were as certain, even dogmatic, about their views as the most fervent bishop in the Church of England. The difference, however, was that the bishop's commitments led to uniformity while the theological approach of Baptists' led to diversity.

What do I mean when I say that Baptists' convictions encouraged theological diversity and ultimately religious liberty and the separation of church and state? Recently I encountered a gripping and felicitous phrase in Charles Talbert's commentary on Luke's Gospel. Writing about the parable of The Good Samaritan, Talbert quoted W. A. Beardslee who spoke of "The way the world comes together again through the parables."[14] If you want to know "how the world came together" for Jesus, you have to read his parables. If you want to know "how the world came together" for disciples of Jesus, you have to read the parables. "How the world comes together!" Simple but descriptive words.

"How the world came together" for Baptists—their inner life, their thought processes, their inner spiritual world—in the seventeenth century issued in freedom of conscience. Baptists grounded their lives in a view of the world that led inevitably to soul liberty. Their commitment to religious liberty and separation of church and state did not come simply from their historical circumstances of adversity. Indeed, had Baptists never felt the sting of religious and civil oppression, the distinct way "the world came together," if logically followed, would have still led to religious liberty and separation of church and state.

Of course, Baptists are as riddled by sin as any group that ever lived. We are as liable to conscript the Bible and theology in the service of self-interest as anybody. Baptists have been, vulnerable, therefore, to build their case for religious freedom on mere expediency. At times they have done exactly that. Indeed, what worries one about some contemporary Baptists in America is that principle has been sacrificed upon the altar of expediency.

It is easy to "holler" freedom when you are the one who does not have it. It is a more principled position, however, to cry for freedom when you are in the majority but now lift your voice on behalf of new minorities. All of Baptists' moral shortfalls notwithstanding, when one reads the historical record of Baptists whole, one sees that Baptists committed themselves to ideas that compelled them to plead for religious liberty and separation of church and state on the basis of principle, not expediency.

How **did** "the world come together for Baptists"? Very quickly, I want to approach the topic from five directions, all of which overlap and all five of which state why Baptists "got that way" on religious liberty and separation of church and state.

First, how did the world come together for Baptists biblically? That is, how did they read their Bibles?

Second, how did the world come together for Baptists theologically? How did they think about God and humanity?

Third, how did the world come together for Baptists ecclesiologically? How did they think about the church?

Fourth, how did the world come together for Baptists philosophically? With what kind of common sense did they approach life in general?

And fifth, how did the world come together for Baptists historically? How did they read human history? Baptists planted their convictions concerning religious liberty in all five soils. A brief word about each of the five.

First, Baptists called for religious freedom because of the way they read the Bible. Like all people Baptists went to the Bible with lenses that refracted the truth of God to them in a certain way. Leon McBeth pointed out that seventeenth-century Anglicans tended to read church-state issues in light of the Old Testament. They liked, for example, the king motif in the history of Israel. Even some Separatists, such as John Robinson, spoke of the godly magistrate and the magistrate's authority to punish religious error, basing this on the power of Old Testament kings. Baptists, on the other hand, spent almost all their time interpreting the New Testament.

Baptists, for example, went to the New Testament to persuade others of the separation of the civil and spiritual kingdoms. Advocating religious liberty never meant that Baptists denied proper authority to civil rulers. In fact, Baptists were Romans 13 people, fond of quoting, "Let every person be subject to the governing authorities." McBeth was right when he said, "The fact that many Englishmen associated Baptists with . . . Anabaptists who disdained magistracy, plus the thought that spiritual liberty would lead to political anarchy, helps explain the frequent and insistent professions of civil loyalty by Baptists."[15]

But Baptists saw two spheres in the Bible. Romans 13 was for the civil, but James 4:12—"There is one lawgiver and judge"—that is, the Lordship of Christ, was for the church. Thomas Helwys in *The Mistery of Iniquity* clearly set out the concept of the two spheres, civil and spiritual. He used Luke 20:25 as his proof text and said he was willing to render obedience to Caesar in matters of the temporal order but he added, "Farr be it from the King to take from Christ Jesus anie one part of that power & honor which belongs to Christ in his kingdome."[16] Roger Williams used this two-spheres model in his famous ship metaphor.[17]

Another favorite biblical text for Baptists was Matthew 13:24-30, the parable about the tares and the wheat growing together. Both should be tolerated until the judgment day, they argued.[18]

Moreover, Baptists said the apostles did not use force but they endured scourging and stonings and the like. The worst they did to those who would not receive the gospel was to shake the dust off their feet (Mt 10:14; Lk 10:11; Acts 13:51).[19] Also, the New Testament, said Baptists, stressed that we are not to lord it over one another (Mk 10:35ff).[20]

Second, Baptists called for religious liberty because of the way the world came together for them theologically. I mention only three theological themes. Baptists anchored their passion for religious liberty to (1) the nature of God, (2) the nature of humanity, and (3) the nature of faith.

Religious freedom, said the early Baptists, is rooted in the nature of God. A sovereign God who dared to create people as free beings is portrayed in the Bible as a liberating deity. Throughout the Old Testament, God is set against persons and institutions that restricted the freedom of God's people. And the complete thrust of Jesus' ministry was to free people from all that would hold them back from obedience to God. Freedom for Baptists was far more than a constitutional right or a governmental gift. God, not nations or courts or human law, is the ultimate source of liberty.

While early Baptists, especially General Baptists, stressed free will, they also emphasized the sovereignty of God. Richard Overton wrote a satirical and humorous masterpiece in the seventeenth century entitled "The Arraignment of Mr. Persecution." Personifying the practice of religious oppression, Overton placed "Mr. Persecution" on trial. At the preliminary inquest ten persons brought charges. "Mr. Sovereignty of Christ" was the first to testify against Mr. Persecution, saying he was an "arch-traitor" to the rule of Jesus Christ over the consciences of humankind.[21] One can render unto Caesar what belongs to Caesar, but the soul, said Baptists, belongs to God alone.

Baptists also based their call for religious liberty on the biblical view of persons. Created in the image of God, a human being is the crowning work of God's creation (Psalm 8). Human personality is sacred and life's highest value. To deny freedom of conscience to any person is to debase God's creation.

Third, and I think here we come to the essence of how the world came together for them, Baptists insisted on soul liberty because of their understanding of faith and the nature of the spiritual life. "To be authentic," Baptists yelled, "faith must be free." Backus spoke for all the Baptists who had gone before him and all who would come after him: "True Religion is a voluntary obedience to God." Baptists have said it in many ways, but it lies at the heart of how the world comes together for them.

"Where there is no autonomy, there is no authenticity."

"If faith is to be valid, it must be voluntary."

"To cram a creed down a person's throat is rape of the soul."

"The only conversion that counts is conversion by conviction."

Martin E. Marty called it "Baptistification." It is an approach to life that underscores freedom, choice, and voluntarism in matters of faith. This is, in my judgment, the core value of the Baptist people.

Third, Baptists called for religious freedom because of their ecclesiological convictions. "The world came together" for them with a certain view of church. Just as salvation was the work of God but never imposed, the church was the work of the Holy Spirit but one was never coerced in it. Helwys had an ecclesiology, says McBeth, where the church was "primarily spiritual rather than organizational. Response to God was highly personal and individualistic. Not only was it impractical and unscriptural to attempt to legislate such a spiritual relationship, it would be completely impossible to do so."[22] And in the opening paragraph of Leonard Busher's 1614 *Religion's Peace: A Plea for Liberty of Conscience,* Busher argued that the church is created not by being born into it but by being reborn, a matter of personal, spiritual response to God.[23]

In his 1615 Confessional Statement Richard Overton argued that

> Christ allowed full power and authority to his church, assembled together, *cordially* and *unanimously*, to choose persons to bear office in the church. And these and no others are to be included, viz. (the offices), of pastors, of teachers, of elders, of deacons, of sub-ministers, who, by the Word of God, from every part are qualified and approved.[24]

Overton wass arguing against the power of the bishops over the churches, and he was giving a definition of the church as a "gathered church." One of Overton's recurring themes was "the sole authority of Jesus Christ versus ecclesiastical hierarchy."[25]

Fourth, the world came together for Baptists philosophically in a natural and commonsense sort of way. Early Baptists used exceedingly practical arguments in support of their contention for freedom of conscience. Thomas Helwys, for example, claimed that religious persecution was both unnecessary and ineffective. The spiritual kingdom does not need the aid of the state, he said. Moreover, rather than producing religious uniformity and protecting civil loyalty, persecution drives people to do the opposite, confirming them more solidly in their judgments. Forcing religion upon people only makes hypocrites out of them. Another practical issue, said Helwys, one that surely did not set well with the likes of James I, was that civil rulers usually are not spiritually fit to preside over religion.[26]

Listen to this natural rights argument! The use of force in matters of religion, said Busher, "is not only unmerciful, but **unnatural**." Equality in matters of the heart, he contended, was the only path to civil tranquility. Injustice breeds disorder.[27] Further, Leonard Busher argued in *Religion's Peace*, as Thomas Helwys before him, that quite apart from the question of right and wrong, coercion in religion is simply not effective in stamping out heretics. Heresies cannot be killed by fire and sword, Busher said, but only by the word and spirit of God.[28]

In what I take to be a most significant and relatively unknown essay, Glen Stassen in "The Christian Origin of Human Rights," argues that the origin of human rights is not found in the rationalism and individualism of the Enlightenment but in the free churches at the time of the Puritan Revolution, a good half century prior to the Enlightenment.[29] Free churches, Stassen argues, based their arguments on biblical, theological, and rational grounds. While reason was not the primary grounding of the Baptist argument, it was certainly present.

Stassen uses Richard Overton, a sixteenth-century General Baptist, to make his point. In Overton's "The Arraignment of Mr. Persecution," to which I have already referred, Overton had a mock trial for Mr. Persecution. The trial ended with a concluding statement from Justice Reason. Not Justice Bible, mind you, or Justice Theology, or Justice Christ, but Justice Reason! Justice Reason, in his conclusion, says that Mr. Persecution threatens "the general and equal rights and liberties of the common people . . . their native and just liberties in general."[30] Baptists distinguished religious liberty and religious freedom as belonging to all persons as persons and not to Christianity or to people of a particular brand of Christianity.

Grounding the argument for religious liberty in natural reason is important because it gives Christians the opportunity to identify with non-Christians in the struggle for human rights. All of us know the story of how Baptists in America united with those of diverse religious views, many of whom were very rationalistic, to move closer to the ideal of religious liberty.[31] What Stassen observed about human rights in general can be applied to the Baptist drive for religious liberty in particular: "The ethic of human rights can be a universal ethic, not because its *source* is a common philosophy believed by all people but because its *intention and application* affirm the rights of all persons."[32] No wonder Helwys said,

"Let them be heretikes, Turks, Jewes, or whatsoever, it appertynes not to the earthly power to punish them in the least measure."

Fifthly, while not a major argument, Baptists called for religious liberty on the basis of history itself. Busher chided proud, old England by comparing it to Muslim Constantinople. "I read that Jews, Christians, and Turks, are tolerated in Constantinople," he said, "and yet are peaceable, though so contrary the one to the other."[33] And Richard Overton, taking the historical evidence in another direction, pointed to historical examples in Germany, Holland, France, Scotland, and Ireland and asked what caused that civil unrest but "this devilish spirit of binding the conscience?"[34]

So the world came together for Baptists biblically, theologically, ecclesiologically, philosophically, and historically in such a way that it drove them to a "theology of pluralism." Birthed in adversity, Baptist convictions issued in diversity.

Baptists: Engaged in Political Activity

It is obvious from all that I have said that Baptists were far from passive observers in their quest for religious freedom. They got that way on issues of conscience because their convictions issued into activity. To **say** something is one thing; to **act** on what you say is quite another thing. Actions confirm and deepen rhetoric. You believe it more once you do something about it.

Back several years ago when the "Honk if you love Jesus" bumper stickers were popular, I saw a clunker of a car hobbling down the interstate. Bent up, broken down, with several colors of paint on it, and puffing down the road, the bright, new bumper sticker read, "If you love Jesus—Push!" Honking is not enough! Baptists certainly "honked" about religious liberty; they did more than "honk," however.

They lobbied with their lives and pens, and they lobbied **together** as a denomination, not simply as lone individuals howling in the night against the cold winds of constrictionism. When one starts pushing at whatever she is honking about, the thing tends to get positioned firmly in the soul. There was a Baptist Joint Committee long before there was a Joint Committee in 1936. Baptists lobbied jointly with their pens and lives for religious liberty. They even broke laws deliberately and premeditatively.

Thomas Helwys spoke not only for himself, but for his little band of believers when he wrote *The Mistery of Iniquity*. Near the close of his document, Helwys used the plural in more than an editorial way:

> Let none thinke that we are altogether ignorant, what . . . war we take in hand, and that wee have not sitt downe and in some measure throughly considered what the cost and danger may be: and also let none thinke that wee are without sense and feeling of our owne inability to begin, and our weaknes to endure to the end, the weight and danger of such a work: Lett none therefore despise the day of small things.[35]

Let none despise the day of small beginnings, indeed!

In no place in Baptist life does one see political engagement by the entire denomination better than in America in the work of Baptist associations in the eighteenth century. The temptation in Baptist historiography has been to isolate the accomplishments of salient individuals without recognizing and giving due credit to the denominational context within in which the individuals worked. John Leland cannot be understood apart from his work on behalf of associations in both Virginia and New England. Isaac Backus, likewise, cannot be properly appraised apart from the Warren Association.

In its 1791 circular letter the General Committee of Virginia described itself as the "political mouth"[36] of the Baptists of Virginia, a heritage I would suggest that the Baptist Joint committee has perpetuated in grand style. And the Warren Association of Rhode Island adopted in 1769 a "plan to collect grievances" on issues of religious freedom.[37]

The Warren subsequently appointed a personal agent to act for the association. The agent became the voice of the Warren Association on behalf of religious liberty. The first agent was Hezekiah Smith, the incomparable pastor of the Haverhill Baptist church in Haverhill, Massachusetts. The second was John Davis, pastor of the Second Baptist Church in Boston, who was selected to act for "Baptists as a denomination." Had Davis not died suddenly, he might have become one of American Baptists' greatest champions of religious freedom. Immediately before his selection as agent for the Warren Association, Davis had taken a strong stand for religious liberty in Boston. This incident had brought him to the attention of the Warren Association. And except for Davis' sudden death Baptists may have never heard of Isaac Backus as a great activist for religious liberty.

Backus became the third agent of the Warren Association. Most of Backus' treatises and sermons on religious freedom were written after he assumed the office of "agent" of the Warren Association. His petitions, memorial, and remonstrances were usually signed, "Isaac Backus, Agent of the Baptist Churches."

Here is my point: the Baptist fight to disestablish state churches was not a political fray that courageous individuals entered alone; it was a melee in which the entire denomination was involved. Many Baptists in America may have forgotten that it was the struggle for religious liberty and the struggle for an educated ministry that first brought Baptists in America together. Foreign missions is often given that credit, but that is to read later affections back into early Baptist history. Not until William Carey and 1792 did Baptists get together on global missions. Years prior to Carey Baptists had been plugging away for soul liberty.

Interestingly, it is on issues of religious liberty that Baptists of America still cooperate more than they do on any other issue. It has been an ecumenical force for Baptist life for most of Baptist history. Their denominational cooperation in lobbying on behalf of religious liberty and separation of church and state has made them more committed to the concepts for which they lobbied.

Conclusion

Groucho Marx once said, "I didn't like the play, but then I saw it under adverse conditions—the curtain went up!" And so the Baptist people. They did not like what they saw in England and the colonies in the seventeenth and eighteenth centuries, but they had no choice. The curtain had gone up. They were birthed in adversity. That historical experience, plus the way the theological world came together for Baptists and the fact that they would not remain passive in the face of freedoms denied—those were the factors that explain how Baptists "got that way" on issues of the freedom of conscience and separation of church and state.

I would only add of our time: if we love freedom, we are going to have to unite with the Baptist Joint Committee[38] and push—HARD!

Notes

[1]For the U.S. statistics, see Robert Gardner, "Baptist General Bodies in the USA," *Baptist History and Heritage* 31/1 (January 1996): 50.

[2]For world statistics, see *Baptists Around the World*, ed. Albert W. Wardin (Nashville TN: Broadman & Holman Publishers, 1995) 473.

[3]For references in Walker Percy's writings see his following novels, *The Second Coming* (New York: Washington Square Press, 1980) 218; *Love in the Ruins* (New York: Avon Books, 1971) 22; *Thanatos Syndrome* (New York: Farrar, Straus, and Giroux, 1987) 347.

[4]Originally published in 1972 by Broadman Press in Nashville TN, a revised edition was issued in 1995 by Smyth & Helwys Publishing, Inc., of Macon GA.

[5]As cited in H. Leon McBeth, *English Baptist Literature on Religious Liberty to 1689* (New York: Arno Press, 1980) 4. This book, a reprint of McBeth's 1961 doctoral dissertation at Southwestern Baptist Theological Seminary in Ft. Worth TX, is a marvelous resource for the subject at issue.

[6]William L. Lumpkin, *Baptist Confessions of Faith*, Rev. ed. (Valley Forge PA: 1969) 124.

[7]Lumpkin, 140.

[8]H. Leon McBeth, *A Sourcebook For Baptist Heritage* (Nashville TN: Broadman Press, 1990) 72.

[9]McBeth, *English Baptist Literature*, 39.

[10]As cited in McBeth, *A Sourcebook*, 74.

[11]Ibid., 75.

[12]Ibid.

[13]*The Writings of John Leland*, ed. L. F. Greene (New York: Arno Press, 1969) 184.

[14]See Charles H. Talbert, *Reading Luke: A Literary and Theological Commentary on the Third Gospel* (New York: Crossroad, 1988) 124.

[15] McBeth, *English Baptist Literature*, 52.

[16]Cited in Ibid., 33.

[17]See Anson Phelps Stokes, *Church and State in the United States* (New York: Harper & Bros., 1950) 1:197.

[18]Glen H. Stassen, *Just Peacemaking: Transforming Initiatives for Justice and Peace* (Louisville KY: Westminster/John Knox Press, 1992) 146.

[19]Ibid., 147

[20]Ibid., 150.

[21]Ibid., 145.

[22]McBeth, *English Baptist Literature*, 33.

[23]Cited in McBeth, *A Sourcebook*, 73.

[24]Cited in B. Evans, *The Early English Baptists* (London: J. Heaton & Son, 1862) 1:255.

[25] Stassen, 143.

[26] McBeth, *English Baptist Literature*, 37.

[27] McBeth, *A Sourcebook*, 74.

[28] McBeth, *English Baptist Literature*, 44.

[29] While not arguing precisely as does Stassen, E. Glenn Hinson maintains something of the same in James Leo Garrett, Jr., E. Glenn Hinson, and James E. Tull, *Are Southern Baptists "Evangelicals"?* (Macon GA: Mercer University Press, 1983) 178.

[30] Stassen, 148.

[31] Robert T. Handy, "The Principle of Religious Freedom and the Dynamics of Baptist History," *Perspectives in Religious Studies* 13/4 (Winter 1986): 28.

[32] Stassen, 156.

[33] McBeth, *A Sourcebook*, 74.

[34] Stassen, 146.

[35] Cited in McBeth, *English Baptist Literature*, 38.

[36] See Walter B. Shurden, *Associationalism among Baptists in America, 1707–1814* (New York: Arno Press, 1980) 208.

[37] Ibid., 212.

[38] The Baptist Joint Committee (BJC) is referred to several times in this book. Established in 1936, the BJC is a Baptist watchdog agency in Washington DC and deals exclusively with issues of religious liberty and the separation of church and state. The BJC is composed of representatives from various national cooperating Baptist bodies in the United States. Of the larger Baptist bodies in America, only the Southern Baptist Convention is not affiliated with the BJC.

The Baptist Vision of Religious Liberty

James M. Dunn

> Then God said, "Let us make humankind in our image, according to our likeness; and let them have dominion over the fish of the sea, and over the birds of the air, and over the cattle, and over all the wild animals of the earth, and over every creeping thing that creeps upon the earth."
> So God created humankind in his image, in the image of God he created them; male and female he created them.
> (Genesis 1:26-27)

Drop a pebble in a pond. Watch the ripples. Concentric circles go out from the center. That spot takes on life. Energy emanates.

That little snapshot symbolizes the Baptist vision of religious liberty. It is a dynamic vision; there is nothing static about it. Baptists see religious liberty as springing from and directly related to the center of the divine-human encounter.

Soul Freedom

Using this pebble-in-the-pond graphic, see the point of impact as the investment of the divine image in all humankind. It is the moment Michelangelo captured with God touching the finger of the first human being. The center circle represents that point of contact.

Genesis 1:26-27 is not a bad place to start. "Then God said, 'Let us make humankind in our image, according to our likeness; and let them have dominion over the fish of the sea, and over the birds of the air, and over the cattle, and over all the wild animals of the earth, and over every creeping thing that creeps upon the earth. So God created humankind in his image, in the image of God he created them; male and female he created them.' "

No matter how one reads the Genesis account, it clearly suggests that we mere mortals are moral beings, capable of responding to God. The Adam and Eve story makes no sense at all if actual response to the Creator was not possible.

Whether one's look at Genesis is the most literal or the most liberal, human beings are able to respond to God. Response–able. Responsible! See where that word came from. If all earthlings are responsible, a certain freedom follows.

That freedom we Baptists call soul freedom. It precedes and goes beyond the Reformation's concept of the priesthood of all believers. Soul freedom is universal. It is the inherent dimension of humanity that invests dignity and worth.

The late F. J. Sheed wrote, "In the Christian view, being a man is itself so vast a thing, that the natural inequalities from one man to the next are a trifle by comparison."[1] Forgive the brother for being born before genderless language, but his point is clear. Maybe we should be reminded by Dorothy L. Sayers' probing essays, "Are Women Human?"[2] that being human is "the vast thing."

Soul freedom and the concept of free moral agency from the Baptist point of view finds our volitional capacity written into our being. We are programmed to be choosers. Our software requires it.

The freedom-responsibility aspect of human nature is like a coin, no matter how thin it's sliced it still has both sides. The faces of the free moral agency coin are indissolubly joined. Every freedom, every decision, every deliberate direction taken has certain consequences and invokes some level of responsibility. Every responsibility, every "oughtness," every duty implies some freedom to choose. God did not make puppets, automatons, but persons in the divine image.

Still, in the first small circle, if the pebble dropped in the pond represents the way the Creator meant for us to be, the debates on the divine design have filled libraries, plagued philosophers and been the excuse for all manner of earthly conflict. The purpose of this modest sally is not to join that battle.

Here one simply argues by assertion that the biblical estimate of humankind is the starting point for understanding religious liberty. If one presupposes creatures made somehow like God—persons, deciders, choosers—then precisely that construction demands freedom.

Every inclusive "whosoever" in the Scripture from Genesis to Revelation suggests not only the personal ability to decide for oneself but a biblical necessity for individual choices. Hear again the closing invitation of Holy Scripture: "The Spirit and the bride say, 'Come.' And let everyone who hears say, 'Come.' And let everyone who is thirsty come. Let anyone *who wishes* take the water of life as a gift" (Rev 22:17, emphasis added).

This assessment of the human condition is a search for the roots of religious liberty. The competence of the individual before God precedes reformation thought because it is rooted, not merely in scripture, but in the nature and being of God. Made in God's image, we can and must respond. Even not to respond is a response.

God made human beings with a faculty no other can control. The "I" at the center of our being even Almighty God will not trample.

For all who practice an experiential religion, the encounter with Jesus Christ finds the image of God, though marred and effaced, restored. Coming to Christ is the defining moment that ripples out, shapes and changes all of life that follows.

The "new creature" in Christ is touched by the finger of God just as Adam was pictured in Michelangelo's Sistine Chapel. The experience of the new birth is not simply another event on the cafeteria line of choices but the hinge in our personal history. In coming to God through Christ, we are becoming who we were meant to be. It is precisely "for freedom Christ has set us free" (Gal 5:1).

And so, Baptists understand soul freedom, value it, and are determined to share it with others.

Religious Liberty

The second circle that ripples out is religious liberty. If the center of the ripples represents the way we are made and made over and if the rock hitting the water pictures the soul freedom invested in every last human being replicating God, then religious liberty is in the first order of consequences.

Soul freedom is the biblical and theological starting point and religious liberty naturally follows. If we all, in some serious way, replicate God, Religious liberty is a moral and social inevitability.

All Christian missions and evangelism and ethics are predicated upon religious liberty. Without religious liberty are ethical choices meaningful? One could say, "yes" to every challenge to "do right," but if saying "no" is not an option what merit are all the yeses?

We invite others to follow Christ with the firm belief that led by God's Spirit they can decide to do so. The whole missionary venture is built upon the assumption (biblically and theologically sound, it seems) that lives can be changed and that folks must freely follow the Lord. If fact, we preach that we come to Christ freely or not really. Coercion makes hypocrites, not believers.

The Bible mandates faithful proclamation of religious liberty. How can anyone experience God and fail to share that relationship? Even so, the freedom fire that burns in the belly of every Baptist cannot be contained.

We can all say, "I have found the Messiah." And because we can, we must. We understand, in our innards at least, that being made in God's image makes us free and responsible. That understanding, however intuitive and visceral, must also be passed along.

The Golden Rule, no less, makes salespeople of all true Baptists for religious liberty. "In everything, do to others as you would have them do to you" (Matt 7:12). If anyone's religious liberty is denied, everyone's religious liberty is endangered. That's not simply a nice slogan. It is the truth! It describes the reality of any people trying to coexist: some slave, some free. If the powers and principalities can deny or try to deny religious liberty to your neighbor, watch out. You may be next.

It's axiomatic then that Baptists care not simply for their own freedom but for the full freedom of religion for all people. We care even, maybe especially, for those with whom we disagree most. That tests our sincerity.

Historically, it has been true. Roger Williams and John Clarke, Baptist founders in Rhode Island, insisted upon opening the colony to all. Jews and Quakers built houses of worship in Newport when no one else would welcome them. Authentic Baptists to this day see religious liberty as a human right. The best brand of Baptists have a track record of defending human rights through the Baptist World Alliance, the United Nations and the ballot box in this country with national leaders of courage and insight.

Baptists have also played an important role in political guarantees for religious liberty. The role of such Baptists in the revolutionary/constitutional period like Samuel Stillman, James Manning, and Isaac Backus needs to be retold and retold. They led the struggle to see to it that the United States would have a Bill of Rights. John Leland joined that fight in Virginia. Can one imagine a preacher wearing the label "Baptist" and not knowing and telling often the story of the these heroes of our freedom. Is it possible that any Baptist pastor would not do the homework necessary to speak with authority on the Baptist contribution to religious liberty? If so, shame! To walk past a sign that says "Baptist" and not proclaim liberty from the pulpit of a church so tagged constitutes false advertising. To fail to be in touch with the tap roots of religious freedom suggests a certain deadness of the Spirit and the spirit of Baptists.

The flame that burns brightly to "proclaim liberty throughout the land to all its inhabitants" (Lev 25:10) is fueled by knowing the Bible, sharing its message, acting out our faith, and loving God's people. Because we live in a specific time and place, because we are citizens of two kingdoms, and because we must find ways to translate love into justice, a dedication to religious liberty needs hands and feet. The essential corollary of religious liberty, therefore, is the separation of church and state.

Separation of Church and State

As certainly as night follows day the third circle out from the center in our preaching pond is church-state separation. It is the logical, theological, and political consequence of a faith that springs from soul freedom and extends religious liberty to all. How can that happen? What must be done with government to assure genuine religious freedom for all? How do a people shape the structures of society to secure liberty?

The founders, heavily influenced by Baptists, were not satisfied with the United States Constitution until a Bill of Rights was added. It may be a stretch to find church-state separation as we know it in the Bible as George W. Truett did. But it's certainly compatible with biblical principles.

Truett, longtime pastor of the First Baptist Church, of Dallas, Texas, preaching on the East steps of the United States Capitol in May, 1920 said,

> To Baptists the New Testament also clearly teaches that Christ's Church is not only a spiritual body but it is also a pure democracy, all its members being equal, a local congregation, and cannot subject itself to any outside control.... In the very nature of the case there must be no union between church and state, because their nature and functions are utterly different. Jesus stated the principle in the two sayings, "My

kingdom is not of this world," and "Render therefore unto Caesar the things which are Caesar's and unto God the things that are God's."[3]

Confusion reigns today around the phrase "separation of church and state." It clearly does not mean separation of God and government. It's not separation of Christians from their citizenship, nor does it mean separation of politics from religion.

Some Baptists fear engagement with the world so much that they would withdraw from contact with the "ungodly." Others have such a triumphal attitude that they think they can use the state to advance God's kingdom. Appropriate distance between the institutions of government and organized religion is to be desired. Separation of church and state has been good for the church and good for the state.

Separation is not neat. It's messy, difficult, inconsistent, and it always has been.

Separation is not obsolete. Today more than ever it is important to apply proper tensions between an invasive, intrusive government and religious institutions which are also concerned with all of life. Government often favors religion when it should leave it alone. Churches appeal for state assistance without counting the cost. When government meddles in religion it always has the touch of mud.

Separation is not complete. Martin Marty suggests that the wall of separation has become a "zone." Stephen Carter sees the wall with "many doors in it." They are probably correct. Yet, somehow there must remain a distinction, a distance even if the wall is no more than a strand of "barbed wire."

One need simply to look at the relationships of church state anywhere else in the world to realize the essentiality of church-state separation to religious liberty. With state churches and church states freedom vanishes. Even with mild and minimal establishment as in the United Kingdom and Scandinavia vital religion is watered down. Without the distance between these two institutions that leaves both free, both suffer.

Neither church not state should be caught in the bear hug of the other. So, perhaps, Truett was right after all, church-state separation may be clearly implied in biblical truth. It certainly flows naturally as a ripple from the impact of soul freedom.

If God made us free and responsible and if God's divine intention is for that liberty to be shared, extended to every soul longing for liberation, then following the biblical design for church and state, both as ordained of God, is the way to go.

Some poet, unknown to me, had it right:

> Let Caesar's dues be paid
> To Caesar and his throne;
> But consciences and souls were made
> To be the Lord's alone.

Notes

[1] As cited in T. B. Maston, *Christianity and World Issues* (New York: Macmillan, 1957) 38.

[2] Dorothy L. Sayers, *Are Women Human?* (Grand Rapids: Wm B. Eerdmans, 1971).

[3] George W. Truett, "See page 69 below."

Religious Liberty
Gift and Opportunity

William H. Brackney

Then God said, "Let us make humankind in our image, according to our likeness; and let them have dominion over the fish of the sea, and over the birds of the air, and over the cattle, and over all the wild animals of the earth, and over every creeping thing that creeps upon the earth." (Genesis 1:26)

But God, who is rich in mercy, out of the great love with which he loved us even when we were dead through our trespasses, made us alive together with Christ—and raised us up with him and seated us with him in the heavenly places in Christ Jesus, so that in the ages to come he might show the immeasurable riches of his grace in kindness toward us in Christ Jesus. For by grace you have been saved through faith, and this is not your own doing; it is the gift of God—not the result of works, so that no one may boast. For we are what he has made us, created in Christ Jesus for good works, which God prepared beforehand to be our way of life.   (Ephesians 2:4–10)

Introduction

We in the Baptist tradition pay a good deal of verbal homage to what we consider a precious historical value, religious liberty. But, do we really understand how vitally important religious liberty is to every facet of our Christian experience? We do well to review regularly what it means to be God's free people and to remind ourselves of the full implications.

Let me begin by asserting that at the core of the freedom we enjoy is the voluntary principle. We act in response to choices. We exercise liberty when we have opportunity. And we serve because we are persuaded that a given service is the most responsible use of our freedom.

We have long exercised our voluntary nature and not known quite what that implies.

The Voluntary Principle in Scripture

We Are Created in God's Image. The writers of Genesis, the Psalms, and the New Testament Gospels and epistles make it abundantly clear that it was God's intention to create in human beings something of His powers to recreate and to make choices. In order to make choices, freedom is absolutely essential. The picture painted in the opening chapters of theological history is of humans who have personal and social freedom, yet who must of necessity make choices. Situation after situation from Cain to Noah to Abram, involves the freedom to make choices. Some people are heroes and heroines of history such as the list recalled in Hebrews 11; others are remembered for poor choices such as Cain, Miriam, Samson, Judas, and the rich young ruler of Matthew 19:16-22. It grieves God our Creator when we make poor choices that bring no honor to God and tend to destroy our prosperity. Yet, we are free to choose and take the consequences.

Religious freedom, then, grows ultimately out of the intentions of Creator God. We are free because this was God's intention for us.

Our Christology exemplifies religious freedom. The writer of the Letter to the Philippians indicates of Christ that he had a moral choice and made it. He was God's equal, yet humbled himself to provide for the redemption of the human race (Phil 2:5-8). He doubtless had the choice of others of his era to pursue his craft or profession, perhaps as a carpenter or a religious teacher, but he chose to become a martyr for his beliefs. And, willingly, Jesus Christ will be part of God's plan to reestablish his kingdom and rule over the earth in the future. Of this much we are certain because of the testimony of Scripture.

The gospel by its very nature is voluntary. It should not surprise us, therefore, that what God offers to us in Christ assumes spiritual freedom and opportunity. Jesus invited all of his early disciples to follow him. Built into the term "follow" is the nuance of "going along with" voluntarily. To some he gave fullness, correction, and meaning in this life; to others he gave healing; and to still others he promised eternal life. His choices were rarely attractive from a human perspective: they involved hard work, defeat, disappointment, persecution, and a good chance of losing one's life. On the other hand, in each case, those called could have chosen to remain as they were. This for me makes the gospel a genuine choice.

And what of the gospel in our own lives? Once having chosen to trust Christ, what is the continued meaning and application of our religious freedom? In the first instance, our liberty is fulfilled in denial of one's self: our Lord said, "If any want to become my followers, let them deny themselves and take up their cross daily and follow me" (Luke 9:23). Our religious liberty is then expressed in its fullest and second *tense* in our opportunity *to do good works* as Paul enjoined his friends at Ephesus (Eph 2:8-9). Again, Jesus exemplified his freedom when it was said of him that "he went about doing good" (Acts 10:38). Our faithfulness depends upon the freedom to follow Christ.

Doing Good Works Fulfills Our Liberty in Christ

The Apostle Paul's argument is this: God has ordained or planned in His providence that we should fulfill His gracious purposes in the world, and that we should do so willingly and voluntarily. He shaped us for this purpose and provided for our salvation in part in this life to this end. A large part of what it means to be conformed to the image of Christ is benevolence.

Now if Paul's logic is accurate, we should enjoy opportunities and resources to do good works. And since we have been remade in Christ, our desire should be heightened, our *voluntariness* should be excited. Indeed this happens to be historically valid. Where there are a predominant number of professing Christians in a culture, there is a concomitant record of human benevolence. This could be illustrated in the case of Victorian Britain, the era of the Second Great Awakening in the United States, or the post-World War II era in North America in general. Countless hundreds of societies, funds, projects, and individual efforts to serve humanity in the name of Christ are a matter of record.

In a recent study of American voluntarism by the Voluntary Sector, Inc., a Washington-based think-tank, some fascinating trends emerged. First, well over ninety percent of Americans gave of their time or financial resources to some type of service organization or church/ synagogue/religious affiliation. Of those who gave, eighty percent also expressed a religious affiliation. The sociologist interprets this to mean that there is a strong correlation therefore between religious convictions and benevolence, or as we might put it, between spiritual values and good works.

The converse of the application of this data is also intriguing. In oppressive societies where the Christian gospel has not taken root or where governments have repressed the churches, there is little benevolence or concern for others. One could list the former Marxist regimes in Europe and Asia, or those states where Buddhism or Hinduism are predominant as largely individual religious expressions. For these very basic reasons, Baptists have been at the forefront of those calling for religious liberty as a basic human and, later, in God's providence, Christian right.

How does this tie in with our heritage of religious liberty? The freedom Christians enjoy in Christ is in large measure a liberty to practice their values. If we believe that human bondage is immoral, we form coalitions to liberate the oppressed. If we affirm a just society for all of its members, we join associations to advocate generous public assistance. If we oppose abuse of disadvantaged persons, we support organizations that expose the abuses. If we believe that the gospel implies a peaceful, nonviolent resolution of conflict, we oppose the use of arms and declarations of military interventions. And most of all, if we believe that true freedom is found only in Christ, we give generously to the advancement of the gospel in mission endeavors. Christian voluntarism is thus realized not just in churchly settings and outreach, but anywhere or every means available to actualize our Christian values. In short, we exercise our religious liberty, we take advantage of our spiritual freedom by being *zealous for good works*.

Religious liberty is a functional reality. We are given the precious liberties we enjoy in order to use them for God's purposes, which in turn bless God and bring us great satisfaction and fulfillment. This is what Paul meant when he asserted that "God desires to show the incomparable riches of his grace" (Eph 2:6).

Religious Freedom and the Work of Others

Religious freedom allows us to accept the gifts and experience of others as well as our own. As we are free in Christ, we recognize that others also belong to Christ and serve him faithfully. Many Baptists from our earliest history have observed that other individuals and groups labor faithfully in the name of the gospel, and sometimes we even cooperate.

Names like Dorothy Hazzard, John Bunyan, Roger Williams, James Manning, Richard Fuller, Walter Rauschenbusch, Helen Barrett Montgomery, Robert G. Torbet, Ernest Payne, Martin Luther King, Jr., and Howard Thurman all worked shoulder to shoulder with persons of differing theological traditions.

It was the great Baptist missionary pioneer William Carey who brought the Christian tradition not only the practical application of the voluntary association for mission purposes, but also an invitation to others of many different persuasions to join with him in the advance of Christ's kingdom. Carey heralded a new era of cooperative missionary endeavor, and in his famous book, *A Solemn Enquiry*, he made the case for cooperation by not only respecting the work of others, but footnoting their strategies for his own organization. Like William Carey, it is our own sense of freedom that allows us this privilege, and it is a telling empowerment by us of other Christians. Across the centuries, Baptists at their best have been free to move about in the Body of Christ.

Mission: The Final Word

Perhaps no other context better illustrates the connection between religious liberty and the voluntary principle than Baptists in mission. In every case where Baptists have pioneered a mission field, they have first demonstrated the need to establish religious freedom. This is so because we hold that evangelism and discipleship cannot take place until, from a human standpoint, the political and social contexts are free. A baptism that is coerced in any way, a faith that is imposed by tradition, or a church relationship that is prescribed by statue, is unacceptable to Baptist Christians.

We could raise the examples of Adoniram and Ann Judson in nineteenth-century Burma, who patiently endured persecution until the government relented and allowed freedom of religion. Or we could adduce the case of Johann Gerhard Oncken, also in the last century, who stood before German magistrates to claim his political freedoms in order to open his culture to a free church. Or, in North America we could recall the experience of the antislave preachers such as William Brisbane, in the North, South, and West who followed the logic that one's soul could not be freed until one's body was free as well.

Baptists do indeed rightly pay homage to our tradition of religious liberty. It is inherent in who we believe human beings are under God and can become in Christ. Made in the image of God, created in Christ Jesus to do good works, we dare not be otherwise. May God enable us to be faithful to these truths and to be courageous in proclaiming our liberty in Christ.

Freedom is a State of Mind

Carolyn DeArmond Blevins

Then the Lord spoke to Moses, "Go and tell Pharaoh king of Egypt to let the Israelites go out of his land." But Moses spoke to the Lord, "The Israelites have not listened to me; how then shall Pharaoh listen to me; poor speaker that I am?" Thus the Lord spoke to Moses and Aaron, and gave them orders regarding the Israelites and Pharaoh king of Egypt, charging them to free the Israelites from the land of Egypt. (Exodus 6:10-13)

Charlie Anderson knew trouble when he saw it. Here he was, a father of six sons and one daughter, caught in the Shenandoah valley of Virginia in the middle of one giant struggle—the struggle between the Union and the Confederacy. With six sons of fighting age the conflict landed squarely by the fireside in the parlor of Anderson's home: "Should slaves be free? Would you give your life or the life of your son for that cause?" The Broadway musical *Shenandoah* depicts this national issue as it comes home to the Anderson family. Two youngsters of the community, a slave boy and Anderson's youngest son, give voice to the struggle as they sing quite simply but profoundly, "Freedom is a flame that burns within ya, Freedom's in the state of mind."

Freedom is a state of mind? One can imagine both boys' grandfathers shouting from their graves, "Forget that foolishness about freedom being a state of mind." A slave boy's grandpa would have likely said, "Freedom is not being sold by one owner to another." A white boy's grandpa in Virginia might have said, "Freedom is preaching without being thrown in jail." Freedom for Americans, slave and free, meant untying the constraints that made life miserable.

Yet the two young boys get beyond the daily realities of freedom to the core of it: freedom is in the state of mind. Freedom is an attitude. Is freedom about laws? Is liberty about rights? Sure it is. But where do laws and rights originate? In the minds or attitudes of those who govern! Freedom IS a flame that burns within you—it IS in a state of mind.

Religious Freedom is also in a state of mind; it is an attitude. Prohibiting religious freedom reflects an attitude of restriction and control. Permitting religious liberty reflects an attitude that values voluntary religion. Either response to religious freedom exhibits an attitude or state of mind. We want laws protecting religious freedom. We demand the right to worship as we please. But laws and rights will be riddled with loopholes that weaken them unless religious freedom is firmly embedded in the mind. Religious freedom is a commitment that goes much deeper than laws and rights. When did this state of mind regarding religious freedom begin?

Religious Freedom: Rooted in the Bible

Freedom of religion is not new; it did not originate in America. Religious freedom is biblical; it came with the divine act of creation. God gave freedom of religion to the created ones. God never forced faith on anyone! God created all people and later created the Hebrew nation. More than once God rescued the Jews. Like a patient parent God forgave them many more times than they deserved. In spite of God's generosity and overwhelming love toward them, they repeatedly rejected the Source of their own existence. Yet the worship of God was never forced on them. From the beginning God, the Creator, gave those persons created in the divine image a choice to worship or reject the very One who gave them life. The Bible is full of stories of people who rejected God. To turn their backs on God was their choice, a choice that God never, even in the gravest circumstances, denied.

One of the most dramatic and exciting stories in the Bible is the exodus, the account of Moses leading thousands of Jewish slaves from Egypt to freedom. For centuries freedom was the impossible dream of the Israelites. No doubt many of them had given up on ever being free again. As Moses wore Pharaoh down, the Israelites' hopes rose, hopes that they might actually escape the brutal hands of the Egyptian ruler. Then the impossible happened. Pharaoh agreed! They could go! Quickly they gathered their belongings and made for the border. And it happened! They won the race with Pharaoh and breathed free air for the first time in four hundred years! Free at last! Thank God and Moses and Aaron and Miriam! They were free at last! All was well. Or was it (see Exod 16:2-3)?

No sooner had the Israelites tasted the heady wine of freedom than some of them began to long for the security of the land of slavery. What an ungrateful bunch of folk! Freedom carried with it uncertainties and responsibilities that they were reluctant to accept. Freedom! It was a state of mind that these newly freed slaves did not yet have. As they moved on to Mt. Sinai, God made clearer their responsibilities as free people in this new nation (Ex 19:3-6). God insisted they have only one God, "I am the Lord your God" (Ex 20:2). Yet God never forced that allegiance. Offended and angry, God did not force that allegiance even when the Israelites worshiped other gods. God certainly had the power to remove all of the competition, all the pagan deities. But God knew that the Israelites must choose their God for themselves if their faith was to be authentic.

God did the unimaginable for the Israelites—freed them from slavery. Surely they would respond by worshiping only the God who rescued them so lovingly and powerfully. Only sporadically did they do so. Repeatedly the Hebrew people chose to worship pagan gods. Repeatedly God punished the nation. Repeatedly God forgave them. But the *option to choose* their faith was never removed. Certainly the people of Israel suffered dire consequences for worshiping other gods, but the freedom to do so was, remarkably, never taken away.

Jesus, God in person, never forced God on anyone. He attracted followers. But never did he coerce them. He showed them the way, spelled out the expectations, and then left the decision of discipleship up to each person. Jesus invited Mary Magdalene, Nicodemus, and Zacchaeus to follow his teaching. However, he never compelled them to do life his way. The Pharisees tried to prescribe religion for others, but they failed. Paul encouraged people to follow Christ's teaching, but none of his letters to young churches or young leaders imposed religion. There is no model in the Bible for forcing one's religion on another. The biblical model is clear: healthy, authentic religion must be voluntary. The individual must decide for himself or herself. Religious freedom is biblical.

Three attitudes form the basis of religious freedom. The first attitude is trust—trust that insists that a person is free to choose or reject God. The second attitude is respect—respect that understands that churches are free to serve God first and foremost. The third attitude essential to religious freedom is fairness—fairness that believes that one person or group cannot make religious decisions for another.

Religious Freedom: A Matter of Trust

Religious freedom begins with the essential attitude of trust, insisting that a person is free to accept or reject God. Trust recognizes that every person has the ability and responsibility to make one's own decisions. God gives that ability. As a baby you were given few opportunities to make decisions. The older you got, the more decisions you made. The more your parents trusted you, the more decisions they allowed you to make. Religious freedom trusts that decision-making ability you have developed as a gift from God.

Freedom to decide for yourself is a principle you cherish, at least you think you cherish it until you realize the high cost of freedom. Freedom slaps you in the face sometimes. Remember when you went to a party without your parents for the first time and thought you were so big, only to discover it was a boring party. You wanted to leave, but couldn't blame leaving on your parents? You had to find your own reason for getting away. Or remember when you drove the car for the first time without an adult? Thought you were hot stuff, didn't you? Then you came within inches of colliding with another car and it scared the cockiness out of you? Freedom is absolutely awesome—until you face the responsibility that comes with it. That can be downright scary. If only you could simply manage to have all of the liberties of freedom without the responsibilities!

The problem with freedom is that it involves trust. Freedom trusts people to make decisions for themselves. Trust places confidence in others to face options and make choices. More importantly trust affirms God as the creator of each of us. You trust another person's ability to make their own decisions because God gave them that ability. Just as God gave you the ability to make decisions God also gave other people that ability, too. Of course, people make mistakes sometimes. Everybody does. At times every person makes a bad decision. You may take your chances on a red light and get hit. You may choose a lousy date. You may make a bad financial decision. You may take on so many responsibilities that your sanity reaches the breaking point. But your freedom to ever have that choice again is not denied. Yet some religious folk think they should make religious choices for people who appear to make poor religious decisions for themselves. What does that attitude say about our understanding of God? Do we believe God created some people who can make their own religious decisions and some who cannot? People may worship in ways you do not understand or approve, but you will not take away their choice for worship if you remember that God created each of them and gave them the choice to make their own decisions. We honor God when we trust those He created to make their own spiritual choices.

Anne Hutchinson was an English woman who moved to the Massachusetts Bay Colony in the seventeenth century. Reared in a preacher's home, Anne was keenly interested in religious matters. People in her new community began to seek her interpretation of John Cotton's sermons. Before long women and men were gathering in Anne's home regularly to listen to her discussions of religious matters. These meetings, however, created increased anxiety among the city's leaders. Anne stressed a doctrine of grace at a time when the Puritans insisted on a doctrine of works. Anne lost the freedom to continue teaching her beliefs. She was placed under house arrest. When she refused to change her teachings, she was excommunicated from the colony.

God gives every person choices, especially in religious matters. Religious freedom is a state of mind and it begins with trust. An attitude of trusting each other to make choices preserves religious freedom for all.

Religious Freedom: A Matter of Respect

A second attitude essential for religious freedom is respect—respect that believes that churches must be free to serve God first. "What an odd statement," you must be thinking. Of course, churches should serve God first. That statement may appear strange until you recall how often churches or religious institutions have been the culprits in denying freedom of worship to other churches.

King James I of England was sure he knew what was best for everyone religiously. So he ordered all English people in the early seventeenth century to worship in the Church of England. If they refused, two choices remained: leave England or be persecuted. In the American colonies Congregationalists denied Quakers and Baptists the freedom to have their own churches in Massachusetts. Episcopalians regularly jailed Methodists and Baptists in Virginia. No doubt some church groups today would readily deny privileges to certain other religious groups if they could. When a religious group is sure it has the truth, it often sets out to get rid of or limit any other group that disagrees with that truth. Unfortunately churches have not always been the guardian of religious freedom unless they wanted to claim it for themselves. Too often churches have been more interested in freedom for themselves than for others.

Problems abound if the church is not free. How can a church serve God if it *first* must answer to a government or religious bosses? Does the church become responsible to God or some designated human authority? Should a church be accountable only to God? All too often religious or civil authorities have insisted churches be accountable to them.

You see, churches can be scary communities of people, especially if they defy those in control. Church folk believe their first allegiance is to God. That allegiance sometimes places the people in conflict with other authorities. Therefore people in power prefer churches that can be controlled. Very early in its regime the Nazi government secured the support of German priests and preachers. Getting the backing of the clergy meant less resistance from the people and at the same time muzzled any protests by the church. German churches found themselves tied to an increasingly brutal and tyrannical government.

Government officials recognize that there is less opposition to their policies regarding civil issues if the church is on their side. Assuring the support of the church is easier if the government controls the churches. In the past some governments have gone to great lengths to control churches in their territory. Many governments around the world today still insist on controlling religion in their country. But how in the world can secular authority know what is best religiously? It doesn't! Secular governments make choices for religion that support the political agenda. Numerous stories can be told of churches weakened by government control.

But political forces are not the only threats to free churches. Powerful churches have used devious means to prohibit the freedom of churches unlike them. State churches in many countries have eliminated their competition by getting laws passed that forbade or made difficult the existence of other congregations. In colonial days state churches in Massachusetts and Virginia made life exceedingly difficult for churches unlike themselves. That problem of majority intolerance of minorities is not limited to the past, however; it is a potentially current problem as well. The Mormon Church in Utah, the Southern Baptist Convention in the southern states, the Roman Catholic Church in Louisiana—all, if left unchecked, may likely inhibit other faiths in subtle but sure ways. The larger and more powerful a denomination becomes, the easier for it to trample on the freedoms of other churches. Because religious power believes it marches as God's army it can be even more fearsome than civil power.

Those in control, whether civil or religious, do not like to contend with congregations who insist that first and foremost they will serve God. No wonder churches frighten people in power. Even if they once possessed it, those who rule can quickly lose the attitude of valuing or respecting other churches, especially if it serves their political purposes to do so. The powers that be do not want to compete with God for the loyalty of church members. They would rather claim the authority to speak for God and use that authority to subject the churches. The question must be raised: why do some people fear religious freedom? What do they lose when churches are free?

Churches are communities of believers that gather to worship God in ways that are meaningful to them. Religious freedom honors those communities and does not dictate who or how they worship. Religious freedom recognizes that the church is accountable only to God for its religious expressions. Religious freedom is an attitude that expresses confidence in the churches to operate without any control by the government or even another religious group or authority.

Religious freedom! It is a state of mind, but it is also a matter of respect. Religious freedom respects churches as communities of faith whose first responsibility is to God.

Religious Freedom: A Matter of Fairness

The third attitude basic to religious freedom is fairness. Fairness acknowledges that one person or group cannot choose God for another. Forced religion does not take. People coerced to practice a religion against their wills end up merely going through the motions to please those making the requirements. Religion "takes" only when a person chooses that faith for himself or herself. So why does generation after generation keep thinking it can force an effective religion?

King James I tried to chose religion for others and failed. Even the Puritans, James' fierce adversaries, tried to dictate religion for others and failed. Some today would eagerly choose God for the rest of us. Some zealous and well-meaning Christians would even give us all of their rules to obey. John Leland, a Virginia Baptist who was known for being outspoken on the issue of religious liberty, said in 1791, "Let every man speak freely without fear, maintain the principles that he believes, worship according to his own faith, either one God, Three Gods, no God, or twenty Gods; and let government protect him in so doing"[1]

Speaking religious convictions without fear is the essence of freedom of religion. When all religious folk are treated fairly, none need to fear voicing cherished beliefs. "Without fear" is what religious freedom is all about. Freedom to select one's own god is the core of religious liberty. God gave the Hebrews that freedom. Should we do less than God on this matter? Leland said all should be free to choose one or three or twenty gods or even no god at all. The Hebrew people certainly made those choices. Even when those choices were poor, God did not force them to worship him. Leland was right. All people must have the opportunity to choose wisely or foolishly. An attitude of fairness must exist.

When any group chooses the proper religion for others, more problems arise than are solved. Which God will be chosen? In what way will that God be worshiped? Which interpretation of that God will be deemed proper? Will one God be chosen, or three or twenty as Leland suggests? Or will the stated orthodoxy be no God? Who makes those decisions? And why is their decision any better than others?

God wants each individual's choice, not our choice for them, even when we disagree with them. Taking away their choice assumes that God made a mistake in giving them decision-making privileges, and that we will fix what God messed up. Denying another person the opportunity to choose God, even to misinterpret or reject God, is simply **not fair**! Those denied religious freedom see that unfairness. Those who have that freedom, therefore, must be diligent in their fairness to others.

God gave Anne Hutchinson some religious choices. She alone was responsible for the choices she made. But the Puritans were sure they knew what was best for Anne. So her freedom was denied her. Anne is one of millions in every country, culture, and clime who have been denied freedom. It happened in America in earlier days and can easily happen again if freedom is not carefully guarded.

Freedom IS a flame that burns within ya. Freedom IS in a state of mind. Religious freedom is at its best when it is a state of mind, an attitude of trust, respect, and fairness. Christianity is at its best and most vibrant when every believer accepts the faith willingly and voluntarily.

Notes

[1] John Leland, "The Right of Conscience Inalienable," (1791) as reprinted in H. Leon McBeth, ed. *A Sourcebook of Baptist Heritage* (Nashville: Broadman Press, 1990) 180.

The Christian and the State

Roger Hayden

Thus says the Lord to his anointed, to Cyrus, whose right hand I have grasped to subdue nations before him and strip kings of their robes, to open doors before him—and the gates shall not be closed: I will go before you and level the mountains, I will break in pieces the doors of bronze and cut through the bars of iron, I will give you the treasures of darkness and riches hidden in secret places, so that you may know that it is I, the Lord, the God of Israel, who call you by your name. For the sake of my servant Jacob, and Israel my chosen, I call you by your name, I surname you, though you do not know me. I am the Lord, and there is no other; besides me there is no god. I arm you, though you do not know me, so that they may know, from the rising of the sun and from the west, that there is no one besides me; I am the Lord, and there is no other. I form light and create darkness, I make weal and create woe; I the Lord do all these things.

(Isaiah 45:1–7)

Let every person be subject to the governing authorities; for there is no authority except from God, and those authorities that exist have been instituted by God. Therefore whoever resists authority resists what God has appointed, and those who resist will incur judgment. For rulers are not a terror to good conduct, but to bad. Do you wish to have no fear of the authority? Then do what is good, and you will receive its approval; for it is God's servant for your good. But if you do what is wrong, you should be afraid, for the authority does not bear the sword in vain! It is the servant of God to execute wrath on the wrong-doer. Therefore one must be subject, not only because of wrath but also because of conscience. For the same reason you also pay taxes, for the authorities are God's servants, busy with this very thing. Pay to all what is due them—taxes to whom taxes are due, revenue to whom revenue is due, respect to whom respect is due, honor to whom honor is due. Owe no one anything, except to love one another; for the one who loves another has fulfilled the law. The commandments, "You shall not commit adultery; You shall not murder; You shall not steal; You shall not covet"; and any other commandment, are summed up in this word, "Love your neighbor as yourself." Love does no wrong to a neighbor; therefore, love is the fulfilling of the law. Besides this, you know what time it is, how it is now the moment for you to wake from sleep. For salvation is nearer to us now than when we became believers. (Romans 13:1-11)

Then the Pharisees went and plotted to entrap him in what he said. So they sent their disciples to him, along with the Herodians, saying, "Teacher, we know that you are sincere, and teach the way of God in accordance with truth, and show deference to no one; for you do not regard people with partiality. Tell us, then, what you think. Is it lawful to pay taxes to the emperor, or not?" But Jesus, aware of their malice, said, "Why are you putting me to the test, you hypocrites? Show me the coin used for the tax." And they brought him a denarius. Then he said to them, "Whose head is this, and whose title?" They answered, "The emperor's." Then he said to them, "Give therefore to the emperor the things that are the emperor's, and to God the things that are God's." When they heard this, they were amazed; and they left him and went away. (Matthew 22:15-22)

Introduction

God's help comes from the most unexpected quarters! And at times it comes from those who are not always aware that they are doing God's will. Cyrus, the Persian conqueror of the Middle East, six hundred years before Christ, was one such person. The Bible gives not one moral or religious qualification of this Gentile emperor for him to be called, "the Lord's anointed." Cyrus did not know the Lord. Cyrus put a different interpretation upon events, as witness the monuments and inscriptions he erected, but God declared that it was He who "armed" Cyrus, "though you do not know me" (Isa 45:5). But it was "for the sake of . . . Israel my chosen," that God called Cyrus, personally, and gave him the title of messiah. God's election, or "calling" of Cyrus, was based neither upon his character nor his faith, but simply upon God's will. This is the impressive message of this passage.

> I am the Lord, and there is no other,
> I form light, and create darkness,
> I make weal and create woe;
> I the Lord do all these things. (Isa 45:6-7)

God is in control of his creation. His declared will and purpose is that Israel will return to its land. Such a political event demanded that the greatest political power of the day, Cyrus, was involved. Therefore, by his prophet Isaiah, the Almighty God declared Cyrus to be his people's deliverer. He called Cyrus by name, gave him his title, even though Cyrus did not know the Lord.

The Bible is convinced that the political potentates, those who control nations, can be the channels for establishing God's kingdom on earth. They *can* be, *not* they always are. This is the reason the early church recognized that the power of the state could be the vehicle of God's rule for good and urged submission to the governing authority as instituted by God, since the ruling authority was "God's servant for your good."

The difficulty of discovering whether the powers that be *are* ordained of God is one of the most critical decisions for Christians today. If "the governing authorities" are *not* of God, how are they to be challenged—with violent or non-violent means? There are no easy answers to such vexing questions.

Paul's conviction that the civil power derived its authority from God came from his Jewish background. Paul knew persecution primarily from Jews—not from Rome. His experiences at Paphos, Thessalonica, Corinth, and Ephesus taught him that the Roman magistrate generally could be relied upon for impartiality. In Jerusalem, it was Paul's appeal to the emperor that kept him safe from the Jewish mob. He urged prayer by Christians for all kings and those in authority. The "authorities are God's servants, busy with this very thing" (Rom 13:6).

Was Paul following Christ's teaching?

The Gospels recognize that Jesus accepted the civil power of his own day. He, unwilling to be taken and made a king (John 6:15), withdrew swiftly from the public scene. He had a member of the zealot party among the Twelve, but had no desire to overthrow Rome's political dominance. When he came as a messiah to Jerusalem, he deliberately chose the "peace symbol"—a donkey, and not a "horse of war." At his trial the Jewish leaders found it impossible to convince the Roman rulers that Jesus was politically dangerous.

Jesus paid his temple tax with a mild protest, indicating to Peter that he did not want to give offense (Matt 17:22-27). The cleansing of the temple challenged the *manner* in which the high priestly family controlled the temple, but *not* their right so to do. He accepted the Sanhedrin and did not demur when Caiaphas put him on oath (Matt 26:63). He acknowledged Roman supremacy, which forced compulsory service on Jews, and he advised his contemporaries to go the second mile (Matt 5:41).

*Jesus insisted that God and the State are **not** identical.* "Give therefore to the emperor the things that are the emperor's, and to God the things that are God's" (Matt 22:21). The coin, with Caesar's image upon it, belongs to the earth. Human beings, with the image of their creator within them, belong to God. Faced with a choice, the disciple's supreme loyalty is to God. Peter thus interpreted Christ when he said, "Whether it is right in God's sight to listen to you rather than to God, you must judge; for we cannot keep from speaking about what we have seen and heard" (Acts 4:20).

Jesus recognized the possibility of the satanic in the state. Jesus wrestled with this possibility in his temptations, where the "prince of darkness" offered to Christ, rule over the world of people. Said Satan, "All these I will give you, if you will fall down and worship me" (Matt 4:9).

Jesus rebutted this himself and later, faced with the ambitious and political request of the sons of Zebedee, replied, "You know that the rulers of the Gentiles lord it over them, and their great ones are tyrants over them" (Matt 20:25). Jesus rejected such "lording" it over people; he rejected "the might is right" mentality, the mere assertion of authority. Power, for power's sake, Jesus declared satanic. He came to serve, *not* to *be* served.

The power of the state *can* be in the service of God's will, but these two are *not* identical. Sometimes the satanic is manifest in the powers that be. Then, the Christian's loyalty is first to God's rule. But until the satanic is clearly identified, "the authorities are in God's service" and to be accepted.

What is the role of the Church in a Nation?

There has been a long history of the alignment of church and state in the nation in the British Isles, although the so-called FREE churches—Methodist, United Reform, Baptist, Society of Friends, and Black led churches—have a history of denying the link. Instead, there has been a demand for religious liberty for all, whether they believe in God or not. In this context, the role of the church must be the pursuit of a good society shaped by Christ's teaching about the Kingdom of God, and within that, the prophetic role of the church is to bring the challenge of the gospel into the debate.

Ghandi defined seven social sins that can destroy a society as:

Politics without principle;
wealth without work;
commerce without morality;
pleasure without conscience;
education without character;
science without humanity;
and worship without sacrifice.

Positively, what kind of a society do Christians seek?

In 1975 Stephen Mayor, an English United Reformed Church minister, published a small book, *Paradise Defined*, and offered some principles for a Christian society that offer a perspective that could help to evaluate the kind of society we seek in the future.[1]

It must be an open society. Christians are not here to sanctify any one particular ordering of society and declare all else as of the devil. Those who marry themselves to a particular spirit of the times will soon be widowed. Christians are concerned to build an open society in which the total separation of church and state is guaranteed, with freedom within that society to argue from conscience what they believe to be best for the city and its citizens.

It must be a society that recognizes sin's reality. Christians must work for a society that demonstrates the truth of power-sharing. All citizens are sinners, so a little power shared is safer than a society where all the power is in one place. The tyrannies of dictators, from the political left or right, are to be resisted. The reality of humankind's inhumanity to each other is so obvious in our world that we must curb the reality of evil in society by creating shared social structures that will curb evil's power. Evil is a reality, and all that is needed for evil to flourish is that good people do nothing.

It must be a society that does not shirk dealing with collective sins. If the Marxist critique of society had anything to teach us, surely it was this: that there can be whole systems of political power and economic practice that are in the end contrary to the interests of society as a whole. If there is to be hope, then such systems and structures have to be challenged, modified and changed. In this sense Christians must look for a society that is concerned with justice *and* righteousness, a society that faces the politics of caring for humankind not only locally, but nationally and internationally.

It must be a society that knows the proper place of Law. Law is good for society and a necessary safety net in a sinful society. To change the metaphor, law should always be the starting line, rarely if ever, the finishing post. A society built upon a rigid legalism that leaves no place for tempering justice with mercy finds itself facing the absurdity in America of so-called "three strikes" sentencing, or in the United Kingdom of the rigor of the criteria for asylum seekers. Christians seek in society a proper place for law, but also look beyond law to the tasks prescribed by love, both human and divine.

We have to admit, however, that many today are characterized by a sense of powerlessness,. They wrestle with their perceived lack of status, their inability to make decisions that determine their future, and, as a consequence, take few initiatives. To oil the complexity of human relationships a society needs forgiveness, if all people are to work for the good of everyone. Forgiveness provides the possibility of restoring relationships that have broken down.

These things are the essence of the Kingdom of God, which Jesus inaugurated and challenges every generation of his followers to bring to fruition here on earth. It was, Christians believe, because God so loved the world, that in Jesus he embraced the whole of humanity in the complexity of its relationships, and by his death and resurrection declared to all that He is a God who forgives sinners, restores relationships, and calls his followers to demonstrate this good news through service of others and a ministry of reconciliation. As the Christian community we have to join with all who love and care for society.

Conclusion

The words of the Lord through the prophet Jeremiah (29:7,11) to the exiled Israelites in Babylon are pertinent:

> But seek the welfare of the city where I have sent you into exile, and pray to the Lord on its behalf, for in its welfare you will find your welfare. . . . For surely I know the plans I have for you...plans for your welfare and not for harm, to give you a future with hope.

Christians around the world live in a great variety of social systems —capitalist, socialist, totalitarian, tribal, and despotic regimes. The point of tension arises when the system denies liberty of worship and belief. The crown rights of the Redeemer are threatened when "a church free from state control" is denied.

This has been an essential part of our Baptist witness over the centuries. Thomas Helwys, Roger Williams, and in our own day the Russian, Georgi Vins, have all echoed the historic words of Helwys:

> For mens religion . . . is betwixt God and themselves; the king shall not answer for it, neither may the king be judge betwene God and man. Let them be heretikess, Turks, Jewes, or whatsoever, it apperteynes *not* to the earthly power to punish them in the least measure.[2]

We recognize that God is in control of the nations, even those who repudiate Him. He can cause even the wrath of human beings to praise Him. Our task is to pray for the nations, and the peace of humankind is our goal. Our ultimate loyalty is to God's will and purpose, and this is best understood by a complete separation of Church and State. The way to this objective is love. "Love your neighbor as yourself. Love does no wrong to a neighbor," Paul concludes, "therefore, love is the fulfilling of the law" (Rom 13:9-10).

Notes

[1] Stephen Mayor, *Paradise Defined: The Nature of Christian Society* (London: SPCK, 1975) 35-110.

[2] Thomas Helwys, "The Mistery of Iniquity," (1612) as cited in H. Leon McBeth, ed., *A Sourcebook for Baptist Heritage* (Nashville: Broadman, 1990) 72.

Baptists and Religious Liberty

George W. Truett

[*This address was delivered from the east steps of the national capitol at Washington DC, on Sunday, 16 May 1920, in connection with the annual session of the Southern Baptist Convention and at the request of the Baptist churches of Washington. See pages 5-6 of the Introduction to this volume for further help in interpreting this sermon.*]

Southern Baptists count it a high privilege to hold their annual convention this year in the national capital, and they count it one of life's highest privileges to be the citizens of our one great, united country.

> Grand in her rivers and her rills,
> Grand in her woods and templed hills;
> Grand in the wealth that glory yields,
> Illustrious dead, historic fields;
> Grand in her past, her present grand,
> In sunlit skies, in fruitful land:
> Grand in her strength on land and sea.
> Grand in religious liberty.

It behooves us often to look backward as well as forward. We should be stronger and braver if we thought oftener of the epic days and deeds of our beloved and immortal dead. The occasional backward look would give us poise and patience and courage and fearlessness and faith. The ancient Hebrew teachers and leaders had a genius for looking backward to the days and deeds of their mighty dead. They never wearied of chanting the praises of Abraham and Isaac and Jacob, of Moses and Joshua and Samuel; and thus did they bring to bear upon the living the inspiring memories of the noble actors and deeds of bygone days. Often such a cry as this rang in their ears: "Look unto the rock whence ye are hewn, and to the hole of the pit whence ye are digged. Look unto

Abraham your father, and unto Sarah that bare you: for I called him alone, and blessed him, and increased him."

The Doctrine of Religious Liberty

We shall do well, both as citizens and as Christians, if we will hark back to the chief actors and lessons in the early and epoch–making struggles of this great Western democracy, for the full establishment of civil and religious liberty—back to the days of Washington and Jefferson and Madison, and back to the days of our Baptist ancestors, who have paid such a great price, through the long generations, that liberty, both religious and civil, might have free course and be glorified everywhere.

Years ago, at a notable dinner in London, that world–famed statesman, John Bright, asked an American statesman, himself a Baptist, the noble Dr. J. L. M. Curry, "What distinct contribution has your America made to the science of government?" To that question Dr. Curry replied: "The doctrine of religious liberty." After a moment's reflection, Mr. Bright made the worthy reply: "It was a tremendous contribution."

Supreme Contribution of New World

Indeed, the supreme contribution of the new world to the old is the contribution of religious liberty. This is the chiefest contribution that America has thus far made to civilization. And historic justice compels me to say that it was preeminently a Baptist contribution. The impartial historian, whether in the past, present or future, will ever agree with our American historian, Mr. Bancroft, when he says: "Freedom of conscience, unlimited freedom of mind, was from the first the trophy of the Baptists." And such historian will concur with the noble John Locke who said: "The Baptists were the first propounders of absolute liberty, just and true liberty, equal and impartial liberty." Ringing testimonies like these might be multiplied indefinitely.

Not Toleration, But Right

Baptists have one consistent record concerning liberty throughout all their long and eventful history. They have never been a party to oppression of conscience. They have forever been the unwavering champions of liberty, both religious and civil. Their contention now is, and has been, and, please God, must ever be, that it is the natural and fundamental and indefeasible right of every human being to worship God or not, according to the dictates of conscience, and, as long as one does not infringe upon the rights of others, one is to be held accountable alone to God for all religious beliefs and practices. Our contention is not for mere toleration, but for absolute liberty. There is a wide difference between toleration and liberty. Toleration implies that somebody falsely claims the right to tolerate. Toleration is a concession, while liberty is a right. Toleration is a matter of expediency, while liberty is a matter of principle. Toleration is a gift from human beings, while liberty is a gift from God. It is the consistent and insistent contention of our Baptist people, always and everywhere, that religion must be forever voluntary and uncoerced, and that it is not the prerogative of any power, whether civil or ecclesiastical, to compel people to conform to any religious creed or form of worship, or to pay taxes for the support of a religious organization to which they do not belong and in whose creed they do not believe. God wants free worshipers and no other kind.

A Fundamental Principle

What is the explanation of this consistent and notably praiseworthy record of our plain Baptist people in the realm of religious liberty? The answer is at hand. It is not because Baptists are inherently better than their neighbors—we would make no such arrogant claim. Happy are our Baptist people to live side by side with their neighbors of other Christian communions, and to have glorious Christian fellowship with such neighbors, and to honor such servants of God for their inspiring lives and their noble deeds. From our deepest hearts we pray: "Grace be with all them that love our Lord Jesus Christ in sincerity." The spiritual union of all true believers in Christ is now and ever will be a blessed reality, and such union is deeper and higher and more enduring than any and all forms and rituals and organizations. Whoever believes in Christ as personal Saviour is our brother and sister in the common salvation, whether a member of one communion or of another, or of no communion at all.

How is it, then, that Baptists, more than any other people in the world, have forever been the protagonists of religious liberty, and its compatriot, civil liberty? They did not stumble upon this principle. Their uniform, unyielding and sacrificial advocacy of such principle was not and is not an accident. It is, in a word, because of our essential and fundamental principles. Ideas rule the world. A denomination is molded by its ruling principles, just as a nation is thus molded and just as individual life is thus molded. Our fundamental essential principles have made our Baptist people, of all ages and countries, to be the unyielding protagonists of religious liberty, not only for themselves, but for everybody else as well.

The Fundamental Baptist Principles

Such fact at once provokes the inquire: What are these fundamental Baptist principles that compel Baptists in Europe, in America, in some far–off seagirt island, to be forever contending for unrestricted religious liberty? First of all, and explaining all the rest, is the doctrine of the absolute Lordship of Jesus Christ. That doctrine is for Baptists the dominant fact in all their Christian experience, the nerve center of all their Christian life, the bedrock of all their church policy, the sheet anchor of all their hopes, the climax and crown of all their rejoicings. They say with Paul: "For to this end Christ both died, and rose, and revived, that he might be Lord both of the dead and living."

The Absolute Lordship of Christ

From that germinal conception of the absolute Lordship of Christ, all our Baptist principles emerge. Just as yonder oak came from the acorn, so our many–branched Baptist life came from the cardinal principle of the absolute Lordship of Christ. The Christianity of our Baptist people, from Alpha to Omega, lives and moves and has its whole being in the realm of the doctrine of the Lordship of Christ. "One is your Master, even Christ; and all ye are brethren." Christ is the one head of the church. All authority has been committed unto him, in heaven and on earth, and he must be given the absolute preeminence in all things. One clear note is ever to be sounded concerning him, even this, "Whatsoever he saith unto you, do it."

The Bible Our Rule of Faith and Practice

How shall we find our Christ's will for us? He has revealed it in his Holy Word. The Bible, and the Bible alone, is the rule of faith and practice for Baptists. To them the one standard by which all creeds and conduct and character must be tried is the Word of God. They ask only one question concerning all religious faith and practice, and that question is, "What saith the Word of God?" Not traditions, nor customs, nor councils, nor confessions, nor ecclesiastical formularies, however venerable and pretentious, guide Baptists, but simply and solely the will of Christ as they find it revealed in the New Testament. The immortal B. H. Carroll has thus stated it for us: "The New Testament is the law of Christianity. All the New Testament is the law of Christianity. The New Testament is all the law of Christianity. The New Testament always will be all the law of Christianity."

Baptists hold that this law of Christianity, the Word of God, is the unchangeable and only law of Christ's reign, and that whatever is not found in the law cannot be bound on the consciences of human beings, and that this law is a sacred deposit, an inviolable trust, which Christ's friends are commissioned to guard and perpetuate wherever it may lead and whatever may be the cost of such trusteeship.

Exact Opposite of Catholicism

The Baptist message and the Roman Catholic message are the very antipodes of each other. The Roman Catholic message is sacerdotal, sacramentarian, and ecclesiastical. In its scheme of salvation it magnifies the church, the priest, and the sacraments. The Baptist message is nonsacerdotal, nonsacramentarian, and nonecclesiastical. Its teaching is that the one High Priest for sinful humanity has entered into the holy place for all, that the veil is forever rent in twain, that the mercy seat is uncovered and opened to all, and that the humblest soul in all the world, if only he be penitent, may enter with all boldness and cast himself upon God. The Catholic doctrine of baptismal regeneration and transubstantiation is to the Baptist mind fundamentally subversive of the spiritual realities of the gospel of Christ. Likewise, the Catholic conception of the church, thrusting all its complex and cumbrous machinery between the soul and God, prescribing beliefs, claiming to exercise the power of the keys, and to control the channels of grace—all such lording it over the consciences of people is to the Baptist mind a ghastly tyranny in the realm of the soul and tends to frustrate the grace of God, to destroy freedom of conscience, and to hinder terribly the coming of the Kingdom of God.

Papal Infallibility or the New Testament

That was a memorable hour in the Vatican Council, in 1870, when the dogma of papal infallibility was passed by a majority vote. It is not to be wondered at that the excitement was intense during the discussion of such dogma, and especially when the final vote was announced. You recall that in the midst of all the tenseness and tumult of that excited assemblage, Cardinal Manning stood on an elevated platform, and in the midst of that assemblage and holding in his hand the paper just passed, declaring for the infallibility of the Pope, he said: "Let all the world go to bits and we will reconstruct it on this paper." A Baptist smiles at such an announcement as that, but not in derision and scorn. Although the Baptist is the very antithesis of his Catholic neighbor in religious conceptions and contentions, yet the Baptist will whole-heartedly contend that his Catholic neighbor shall have his candles and incense and sanctus bell and rosary, and whatever else he wishes in the expression of his worship. A Baptist would rise at midnight to plead for absolute religious liberty for his Catholic neighbor, and for his Jewish neighbor, and for everybody else. But what is the answer of a Baptist to the contention made by the Catholic for papal infallibility? Holding aloft a little book, the name of which is the New Testament, and without any hesitation or doubt, the Baptist shouts his battle cry: "Let all the world go to bits and we will reconstruct it on the New Testament."

Direct Individual Approach to God

When we turn to this New Testament, which is Christ's guidebook and law for his people, we find that supreme emphasis is everywhere put upon the individual. The individual is segregated from family, from church, from state, and from society, from dearest earthly friends or institution, and brought into direct, personal dealings with God. Every one must give account of oneself to God. There can be no sponsors or deputies or proxies in such vital matter. Each one must repent for oneself, and believe for oneself, and be baptized for oneself, and answer to God for oneself, both in time and in eternity. The clarion cry of John the Baptist is to the individual.

> Think not to say within yourselves, We have Abraham to our father: for I say unto you, that God is able of these stones to raise up children unto

Abraham. And now also the ax is laid unto the root of the trees: therefore every tree which bringeth not forth good fruit is hewn down, and cast into the fire.

One person can no more repent and believe and obey Christ for another than one can take the other's place at God's judgment bar. Neither persons nor institutions, however dear and powerful, may dare to come between the individual soul and God. "There is . . . one mediator between God and people, the man Christ Jesus." Let the state and the church, let the institution, however dear, and the person, however near, stand aside, and let the individual soul make its own direct and immediate response to God. One is our pontiff, and his name is Jesus. The undelegated sovereignty of Christ makes it forever impossible for his saving grace to be manipulated by any system of human mediation whatsoever.

The right to private judgment is the crown jewel of humanity, and for any person or institution to dare to come between the soul and God is a blasphemous impertinence and a defamation of the crown rights of the Son of God.

Out of these two fundamental principles, the supreme authority of the Scriptures and the right of private judgment, have come all the historic protests in Europe and England and America against unscriptural creeds, polity, and rites, and against the unwarranted and impertinent assumption of religious authority over people's consciences, whether by church or by state. Baptists regard as an enormity any attempt to force the conscience, or to constrain human beings, by outward penalties, to this or that form of religious belief. Persecution may make people hypocrites, but it will not make them Christians.

Infant Baptism Unthinkable

It follows, inevitably, that Baptists are unalterably opposed to every form of sponsorial religion. If I have fellow Christians in this presence today who are the protagonists of infant baptism, they will allow me to say frankly, and certainly I would say it in the most fraternal, Christian spirit, that to Baptists infant baptism is unthinkable from every viewpoint. First of all, Baptists do not find the slightest sanction for infant baptism in the Word of God. That fact, to Baptists, makes infant baptism a most serious question for the consideration of the whole Christian world. Nor is that all. As Baptists see it, infant baptism tends to ritualize Christianity and reduce it to lifeless forms. It tends also and inevitably, as Baptists see it, to secularizing of the church and to the blurring and blotting out of the line of demarcation between the church and the unsaved world.

And since I have thus spoken with unreserved frankness, my honored Pedobaptist friends in the audience will allow me to say that Baptists solemnly believe that infant baptism, with its implications, has flooded the world, and floods it now, with untold evils.

They believe also that it perverts the scriptural symbolism of baptism; that it attempts the impossible tasks of performing an act of religious obedience by proxy, and that since it forestalls the individual initiative of the child, it carries within it the germ of persecution, and lays the predicate for the union of church and state, and that it is a Romish tradition and a cornerstone for the whole system of property throughout the world.

I will speak yet another frank word for my beloved Baptist people, to our cherished fellow Christians who are not Baptists, and that word is that our Baptist people believe that if all the Protestant denominations would once for all put away infant baptism, and come to the full acceptance and faithful practice of New Testament baptism, that the unity of all the non–Catholic Christians in the world would be consummated, and that there would not be left one Roman Catholic church on the face of the earth at the expiration of the comparatively short period of another century.

Surely, in the face of these frank statements, our non–Baptist neighbors may apprehend something of the difficulties compelling Baptists when they are asked to enter into official alliances with those who hold such fundamentally different views from those just indicated. We call God to witness that our Baptist people have an unutterable longing for Christian union, and believe Christian union will come, but we are compelled to insist that if this union is to be real and effective, it must be based upon a better understanding of the Word of God and a more complete loyalty to the will of Christ as revealed in His Word.

The Ordinances are Symbols

Again, to Baptists, the New Testament teaches that salvation through Christ must precede membership to his church, and must precede the observance of the two ordinances in his church, namely, baptism and the Lord's Supper. These ordinances are for the saved and only for the saved.

These two ordinances are not sacramental, but symbolic. They are teaching ordinances, portraying in symbol truths of immeasurable and everlasting moment to humanity. To trifle with these symbols, to pervert their forms, and at the same time to pervert the truths they are designed to symbolize, is indeed a most serious matter. Without ceasing and without wavering, Baptists are, in conscience, compelled to contend that these two teaching ordinances shall be maintained in the churches just as they were placed there in the wisdom and authority of Christ. To change these two meaningful symbols is to change their scriptural intent and content, and thus pervert them, and we solemnly believe, to be the carriers of the most deadly heresies. By our loyalty to Christ, which we hold to be the supreme test of our friendship for him, we must unyieldingly contend for these two ordinances as they were originally given to Christ's churches.

The Church a Pure Democracy

To Baptists, the New Testament also clearly teaches that Christ's church is not only a spiritual body but it is also a pure democracy, all its members being equal, a local congregation, and cannot subject itself to any outside control. Such terms, therefore, as "The American Church," or "The bishop of this city or state," sound strangely incongruous to Baptist ears. In the very nature of the case, also, there must be no union between church and state, because their nature and functions are utterly different. Jesus stated the principle in the two sayings, "My kingdom is not of this world," and "Render therefore unto Caesar the things which are Caesar's, and unto God the things that are God's." Never, anywhere, in any clime, has a true Baptist been willing, for one minute, for the union of church and state, never for a moment.

Every state church on the earth is a spiritual tyranny. And just as long as there is left upon this earth any state church, in any land, the task of Baptists will that long remain unfinished. Their cry has been and is and must ever be this:

> Let Caesar's dues be paid
>   To Caesar and his throne;
> But consciences and souls were made
>   To be the Lord's alone.

A Free Church in a Free State

That utterance of Jesus, "Render therefore unto Caesar the things which are Caesar's, and unto God the things that are God's," is one of the most revolutionary and history-making utterances that ever fell from those lips divine. That utterance, once for all, marked the divorcement of church and state. It marked a new era for the creeds and deeds of men. It was the sunrise gun of a new day, the echoes of which are to go on and on and on until in every land, whether great or small, the doctrine shall have absolute supremacy everywhere of a free church in a free state.

In behalf of our Baptist people I am compelled to say that forgetfulness of the principles that I have just enumerated, in our judgment, explains many of the religious ills that now afflict the world. All went well with the early churches in their earlier days. They were incomparably triumphant days for the Christian faith. Those early disciples of Jesus, without prestige and worldly power, yet aflame with the love of God and the passion of Christ, went out and shook the pagan Roman empire from center to circumference, even in one brief generation. Christ's religion needs no prop of any kind from any worldly source, and to the degree that it is thus supported is a millstone hanged about its neck.

An Incomparable Apostasy

Presently there came an incomparable apostasy in the realm of religion, which shrouded the world in spiritual night through long hundreds of years. Constantine, the emperor, saw something in the religion of Christ's people that awakened his interest, and now we see him uniting religion to the state and marching up the marble steps of the emperor's palace, with the church robed in purple. Thus and there was begun the most baneful misalliance that ever fettered and cursed a suffering world. For long centuries, even from Constantine to Pope Gregory VII, the conflict between church and state waxed stronger and stronger, and the encroachments and usurpations became more deadly and devastating. When Christianity first found its way into the city of the caesars it lived at first in cellars and alleys, but when Constantine crowned the union of church and state, the church was stamped with the impress of the Roman idea and fanned with the spirit of the caesars. Soon we see a pope emerging, who himself became a caesar, and soon a group of councilors may be seen gathered around this pope, and the supreme power of the church is assumed by the pope and his councilors.

The long blighting record of the medieval ages is simply the working out of that idea. The pope ere long assumed to be the monarch of the world, making the astounding claim that all kings and potentates were subject unto him. By and by when Pope Gregory VII appears, better known as Hildebrand, his assumptions are still more astounding. In him the spirit of the Roman church became incarnate and triumphant. He lorded it over parliaments and council chambers, having statesmen to do his bidding, and creating and deposing kings at his will. For example, when the Emperor Henry offended Hildebrand, the latter pronounced against Henry a sentence not only of excommunication but of deposition as emperor, releasing to all Christians from allegiance to him. He made the emperor do penance by standing in the snow with his bare feet at Canossa, and he wrote his famous letter to William the Conqueror to the effect that the state was subordinate to the church, that the power of the state as compared to the church was as the moon compared to the sun.

This explains the famous saying of Bismarck when Chancellor of Germany, to the German parliament: "We shall never go to Canossa again." Whoever favors the authority of the church over the state favors the way to Canossa.

When, in the fullness of time, Columbus discovered America, the pope calmly announced that he would divide the New World into two parts, giving one part to the king of Spain and the other to the king of Portugal. And not only did this great consolidated ecclesiasticism assume to lord it over people's earthly treasures, but they lorded it over people's minds, prescribing what human beings should think and read and write. Nor did such assumption stop with the things of this world, but it laid its hand on the next world, and claimed to have in its possession the keys of the Kingdom of Heaven and the kingdom of purgatory so that it could shut people out of heaven or lift them out of purgatory, thus surpassing in the sweep of its power and in the pride of its autocracy the boldest and most presumptuous ruler that ever sat on a civil throne.

Absolutism vs. Individualism

The student of history cannot fail to observe that through the long years two ideas have been in endless antagonism—the idea of absolutism and the idea of individualism, the idea of autocracy and the idea of democracy. The idea of autocracy is that supreme power is vested in the few, who, in turn, delegate this power to the many. That was the dominant idea of the Roman empire, and upon that idea the caesars built their throne. That idea has found worldwide impression in the realms both civil and ecclesiastical. Often have the two ideas, absolutism versus individualism, autocracy versus democracy, met in battle. Autocracy dared, in the morning of the twentieth century, to crawl out of its ugly lair and proposed to substitute the law of the jungles for the law of human fellowship. For all time to come the hearts of human beings will stand aghast upon every thought of this incomparable death drama, and at the same time they will renew the vow that the few shall not presumptuously tyrannize over the many; that the law of human relationships and not the law of the jungle shall be given supremacy in all human affairs. And until the principle of democracy, rather than the principle of autocracy, shall be regnant in the realm of religion, our mission shall be commanding and unending.

The Reformation Incomplete

The coming of the sixteenth century was the dawning of a new hope for the world. With that century came the Protestant Reformation. Yonder goes Luther with his theses, which he nails over the old church door in Wittenberg, and the echoes of the mighty deed shake the papacy, shake Europe, shake the whole world. Luther was joined by Melancthon and Calvin and Zwingli and other mighty leaders. Just at this point emerges one of the most outstanding anomalies of all history. Although Luther and his compeers protested vigorously against the errors of Rome, yet when these mighty men came out of Rome—and mighty men they were—they brought with them some of the grievous errors of Rome. The Protestant Reformation of the sixteenth century was sadly incomplete—it Luther and his compeers grandly sounded out was a case of arrested development. Although the battle cry of justification by faith alone, yet they retained the doctrine of infant baptism and a state church. They shrank from the logical conclusions of their own theses.

In Zurich there stands a statue in honor of Zwingli, in which he is represented with a Bible in one hand and a sword in the other. That statue was the symbol of the union between church and state. The same statue might have been reared to Luther and his fellow reformers. Luther and Melancthon fastened a state church upon Germany, and Zwingli fastened it upon Switzerland. Knox and his associates fastened it upon Scotland. Henry VIII bound it upon England, where it remains even till this very hour.

These mighty reformers turned out to be persecutors like the papacy before them. Luther unloosed the dogs of persecution against the struggling and faithful Anabaptists. Calvin burned Servetus, and to such awful deed Melancthon gave him approval. Louis XIV revoked the Edict of Nantes, shut the doors of all the Protestant churches, and outlawed the Huguenots. Germany put to death that mighty Baptist leader, Balthaser Hubmaier, while Holland killed her noblest statesman, John of Barneveldt, and condemned to life imprisonment her ablest historian, Hugo Grotius, for conscience' sake. In England, John Bunyan was kept in jail for twelve long, weary years because of his religion, and when we cross the mighty ocean separating the Old World and the New, we find the early pages of American history crimsoned with the stories of religious persecutions. The early colonies of America were the forum of the working out of the most epochal battles that earth ever knew for the triumph of religious and civil liberty.

America and Religious and Civil Liberty

Just a brief glance at the struggle in those early colonies must now suffice us. Yonder in Massachusetts, Henry Dunster, the first president of Harvard, was removed from the presidency because he objected to infant baptism. Roger Williams was banished, John Clarke was put in prison, and they publicly whipped Obadiah Holmes on Boston Common. In Connecticut the lands of our Baptist ancestors were confiscated and their goods sold to build a meeting house and support a preacher of another denomination. In old Virginia, "mother of states and statesmen," the battle for religious and civil liberty was waged all over her nobly historic territory, and the final triumph recorded there was such as to write imperishable glory upon the name of Virginia until the last syllable of recorded time. Fines and imprisonments and persecutions were everywhere in evidence in Virginia for conscience' sake. If you would see a record incomparably interesting, go read the early statutes in Virginia concerning the Established Church and religion, and trace the epic story of the history–making struggles of that early day. If the historic records are to be accredited, those clergymen of the Established Church in Virginia made terrible inroads in collecting fines in Baptist tobacco in that early day. It is quite evident, however, that they did not get all the tobacco.

On and on was the struggle waged by our Baptist forebears for religious liberty in Virginia, in the Carolinas, in Georgia, in Rhode Island and Massachusetts and Connecticut, and elsewhere, with one unyielding contention for unrestricted religious liberty for all, and with never one wavering note. They dared to be odd, to stand alone, to refuse to conform, though it cost them suffering and even life itself. They dared to defy traditions and customs, and deliberately chose the day of non-conformity, even though in many a case it meant a cross. They pleaded and suffered, they offered their protests and remonstrances and memorials, and, thank God, mighty statesmen were won to their contention. Washington and Jefferson and Madison and Patrick Henry, and many others, until at last it was written into our country's constitution that church and state must in this land be forever separate and free, that neither must ever trespass upon the distinctive functions of the other. It was preeminently a Baptist achievement.

A Lonely Struggle

Glad are our Baptist people to pay their grateful tribute to their fellow Christians of other religious communions for all their sympathy and help in this sublime achievement. Candor compels me to repeat that much of the sympathy of other religious leaders in that early struggle was on the side of legalized ecclesiastical privilege. Much of the time were Baptists pitiably lonely in their age–long struggle. We would now and always make our most grateful acknowledgment to any and all who came to the side of our Baptist ancestors, whether early or late, in this destiny-determining struggle. But I take it that every informed person on the subject, of whatever religious faith, will be willing to pay tribute to our Baptist people as being the chief instrumentality in God's hands in winning the battle in America for religious liberty. Do you recall Tennyson's little poem, in which he sets out the history of the seed of freedom? Catch its philosophy:

> Once in a golden hour
>   I cast to earth a seed,
> Up there came a flower,
>   The people said, a weed.

To and fro they went,
    Through my garden bower,
And muttering discontent,
    Cursed me and my flower.

Then it grew so tall,
    It wore a crown of light,
But thieves from o'er the wall,
    Stole the seed by night.

Sowed it far and wide.
    By every town and tower,
Till all the people cried,
    "Splendid is the flower."

Read my little fable:
    He who runs may read,
Most can grow the flower now,
    For all have got the seed.

Very well, we are very happy for all our fellow religionists of every denomination and creed to have this splendid flower of religious liberty, but you will allow us to remind you that you got the seed in our Baptist garden. We are very happy for you to have it; now let us all make the best of it and the most of it.

The Present Call

And now, my fellow Christians, and fellow citizens, what is the present call to us in connection with the priceless principle of religious liberty? That principle, with all the history and heritage accompanying it, imposes upon us obligations to the last degree meaningful and responsible. Let us today and forever be highly resolved that the principle of religious liberty shall, please God, be preserved inviolate through all our days and the days of those who come after us. Liberty has both its perils and its obligations. We are to see to it that our attitude toward liberty, both religious and civil, both as Christians and as citizens, is an attitude consistent and constructive and worthy. We are to "Render therefore unto Caesar the things which are Caesar's, and unto God the things that are God's." We are members of the two realms, the civil and the religious, and are faithfully to render unto each all that each should receive at our hands; we are to be alertly watchful day and night, that liberty, both religious and civil, shall be nowhere prostituted and mistreated. Every perversion and misuse of liberty tends by that much to jeopardize both church and state.

There comes now the clarion call to us to be the right kind of citizens. Happily, the record of our Baptist people toward civil government has been a record of unfading honor. Their love and loyalty to country have not been put to shame in any land. In the long list of published Tories in connection with the Revolutionary War there was not one Baptist name.

Liberty Not Abused

It behooves us now and ever to see to it that liberty is not abused. Well may we listen to the call of Paul, that mightiest Christian of the long centuries, as he says: "Brothers and sisters, ye have been called unto liberty; only use not your liberty for an occasion to the flesh, but by love serve one another." This ringing declaration should be heard and heeded by every class and condition of people throughout all our wide stretching nation.

It is the word to be heeded by religious teachers, and by editors, and by legislators, and by everybody else. Nowhere is liberty to be used "for an occasion to the flesh." We will take free speech and a free press, with all their excrescences and perils, because of the high meaning of freedom, but we are to set ourselves with all diligence not to use these great privileges in the shaming of liberty. A free press—how often does it pervert its high privilege! Again and again, it may be seen dragging itself through all the sewers of the social order, bringing to light the moral cancers and leprosies of our poor world and glaringly exhibiting them to the gaze even of responsive youth and childhood. The editor's task, whether in the realm of church or state, is an immeasurably responsible one. These editors, side by side with the moral and religious teachers of the country, are so to magnify the ballot box, a free press, free schools, the courts, the majesty of law and reverence for all properly accredited authority that our civilization may not be built on the shifting sands, but on the secure and enduring foundations of righteousness.

Let us remember that lawlessness, wherever found and whatever its form, is as "the pestilence that walketh in darkness" and "the destruction that wasteth at noonday." Let us remember that he who is willing for law to be violated is an offender against the majesty of law as really as he who actually violates law. The spirit of law is the spirit of civilization. Liberty without law is anarchy. Liberty against law is rebellion. Liberty limited by law is the formula of civilization.

Humane and Righteous Laws

Challenging to the highest degree is the call that comes to legislators. They are to see to it continually, in all their legislative efforts, that their supreme concern is for the highest welfare of the people. Laws humane and righteous are to be fashioned and then to be faithfully regarded. People are playing with fire if they lightly fashion their country's laws and then trifle in their obedience to such laws. Indeed, all citizens, the humblest and the most prominent alike, are called to give their best thought to the maintenance of righteousness everywhere. Much truth is there in the widely quoted saying: "Our country is afflicted with the bad citizenship of good men." The saying points its own clear lesson. "When the righteous are in authority, the people rejoice, but when the wicked bear rule, the people mourn." The people, all the people, are inexorably responsible for the laws, the ideals, and the spirit that are necessary for making of a great and enduring civilization. Every one of us is to remember that it is righteousness that exalteth a nation, and that it is sin that reproaches and destroys a nation.

God does not raise up a nation to go strutting selfishly, forgetful of the high interests of humanity. National selfishness leads to destruction as truly as does individual selfishness. Nations can no more live to themselves than can individuals. Humanity is bound up together in the big bundle of life. The world is now one big neighborhood. There are no longer any hermit nations. National isolation is no longer possible in the earth. The markets of the world instantly register every commercial change. An earthquake in Asia is at once registered in Washington City. The people on one side of the world may not dare to be indifferent to the people on the other side. Every one of us is called to be a world citizen, and to think and act in world terms. The nation that insists upon asking that old murderous question of Cain, "Am I my brother's keeper?" the question of the profiteer and the question of the slacker, is a nation marked for decay and doom and death. The parable of the Good Samaritan is Heaven's law for nations as well as for individuals. Some things are worth dying for, and if they are worth dying for they are worth living for. The poet was right when he sang:

> Though love repine and reason chafe,
>   There comes a voice without reply,
> 'Tis man's perdition to be safe,
>   When for the truth he ought to die.

Things Worth Dying For

When this nation went into the world war a little while ago, after her long and patient and fruitless effort to find another way of conserving righteousness, the note was sounded in every nook and corner of our country that some things in this world are worth dying for, and if they are worth dying for they are worth living for. What are some of the things worth dying for? The sanctity of womanhood is worth dying for. The safety of childhood is worth dying for; and when Germany put to death that first helpless Belgian child, she was marked for defeat and doom. The integrity of one's country is worth dying for. And, please God, the freedom and honor of the United States of America are worth dying for. If the great things of life are worth dying for, they are surely worth living for. Our great country may not dare to isolate herself from all the rest of the world, and selfishly say: "We propose to live and to die to ourselves, leaving all the other nations with their weaknesses and burdens and sufferings to go their ways without our help." This nation cannot pursue any such policy and expect the favor of God. Myriads of voices, both from the living and the dead, summon us to a higher and better way. Happy am I to believe that God has his prophets not only in the pupils of the churches but also in the schoolrooms, in the editor's chair, in the halls of legislation, in the marts of commerce, in the realms of literature. Tennyson was a prophet when, in "Locksley Hall," he sang:

> For I dipt into the future, far as human eye could see,
> Saw the Vision of the world, and all the wonder that would be;
> Saw the heavens fill with commerce, argosies of magic sails,
> Pilots of the purple twilight, dropping down with costly bales;
> Heard the heavens fill with shouting,
>   and there rain'd a ghastly dew
> From the nations' airy navies grappling in the central blue;
> Far along the world–wide whisper of the south–wind rushing warm,

With the standards of the people plunging thro' the thunder-storm.
Till the war drum throbb'd no longer, and the battle-flags were furled
In the Parliament of man, the Federation of the world.

A League of Nations

Tennyson believed in a league of nations, and well might he so believe, because God is on his righteous throne, and inflexible are his purposes touching righteousness and peace for a weary, sinning, suffering, dying world. Standing here today on the steps of our nation's Capitol, hard by the chamber of the Senate of the United States, I dare to say as a citizen and as a Christian teacher, that the moral forces of the United States of America, without regard to political parties, will never rest until there is a worthy League of Nations. I dare to express also the unhesitating belief that the unquestioned majorities of both great political parties in this country regard the delay in the working out of a League of Nations as a national and worldwide tragedy.

The moral and religious forces of this country could not be supine and inactive as long as the saloon, the chief rendezvous of small politicians, that chronic criminal and standing anachronism of our modern civilization, was legally sponsored by the state. I can certify all the politicians of all the political parties that the legalized saloon has gone from American life, and gone to stay. Likewise, I can certify the politicians of all political parties, without any reference to partisan politics, that the same moral and religious forces of this country, because of the inexorable moral issues involved, cannot be silent and will not be silent until there is put forth a League of Nations that will strive with all its might to put an end to the diabolism and measureless horrors of war. I thank God that the stricken man yonder in the White House has pleaded long and is pleading yet that our nation will take her full part with the others for the bringing in of that blessed day when wars shall cease to the ends of the earth.

The recent world war calls to us with a voice surpassingly appealing and responsible. Surely Alfred Noyes voices the true desire for us:

Make firm, O God, the peace our dead have won
    For folly shakes the tinsel on its head,
And points us back to darkness and to hell,
    Cackling, "Beware of visions," while our dead

Still cry, "It was for visions that we fell."

They never knew the secret game of power,
    All that this earth can give they thrust aside,
They crowded all their youth unto an hour,
    And for fleeting dream of right, they died.

Oh, if we fail them in that awful trust,
    How should we bear those voices from the dust?

The Right Kind of Christians

This noble doctrine and heritage of religious liberty calls to us imperiously to be the right kind of Christians. Let us never forget that a democracy, whether civil or religious, has not only its perils, but has also its unescapable obligations. A democracy calls for intelligence. The sure foundations of states must be laid, not in ignorance, but in knowledge. It is of the last importance that those who rule shall be properly trained. In a democracy, a government of the people, for the people, and by the people, the people are the rulers, and the people, all the people, are to be informed and trained.

My fellow Christians, we must hark back to our Christian schools, and see to it that these schools are put on worthy and enduring foundations. A democracy needs more than intelligence, it needs Christ. He is the light of the world, nor is there any other sufficient light for the world. He is the solution of the world's complex questions, the one adequate Helper for its dire needs, the one only sufficient Saviour for our sinning race. Our schools are afresh to take note of this supreme fact, and they are to be fundamentally and aggressively Christian. Wrong education brought on the recent world war. Such education will always lead to disaster.

Pungent were the recent words of Mr. Lloyd George: "The most formidable foe that we had to fight in Germany was not the arsenals of Krupp, but the schools of Germany." The educational center of the world will not longer be in the Old World, but because of the great war, such center will henceforth be in this New World of America. We must build here institutions of learning that will be shot through and through with the principles and motives of Christ, the one Master over all humankind.

The Christian School

The time has come when, as never before, our beloved denomination should worthily go out to its world task as a teaching denomination. That means that there should be a crusade throughout all our borders for the vitalizing and strengthening of our Christian schools. The only complete education, in the nature of the case, is Christian education, because a human being is a tripartite being. By the very genius of our government, education by the state cannot be complete. Wisdom has fled from us if we fail to magnify, and magnify now, our Christian schools. These schools go to the foundation of all the life of the people. They are indispensable to the highest efficiency of the churches. Their inspirational influences are of untold value to the schools conducted by the state, to which schools also we must ever give our best support. It matters very much, do you not agree, who shall be the leaders, and what the standards in the affairs of civil government and in the realm of business life? One recalls the pithy saying of Napoleon to Marshal Ney: "An army of deer led by a lion is better than an army of lions led by a deer." Our Christian schools are to train not only our religious leaders but hosts of our leaders in the civil and business realm as well.

The one transcending inspiring influence in civilization is the Christian religion. By all means, let the teachers and trustees and student bodies of all our Christian schools remember this supremely important fact, that civilization without Christianity is doomed. Let there be no pagan ideals in our Christian schools, and no hesitation or apology for the insistence that the one hope for the individual, the one hope for society, for civilization, is in the Christian religion. If ever the drum beat of duty sounded clearly, it is calling to us now to strengthen and magnify our Christian schools.

The Task of Evangelism

Preceding and accompanying the task of building our Christian schools, we must keep faithfully and practically in mind our primary task of evangelism, the work of winning souls from sin unto salvation, from Satan unto God. This work takes precedence of all other work in the Christian program. Salvation for sinners is through Jesus Christ alone, nor is there any other name or way under heaven whereby they may be saved. Our churches, our schools, our religious papers, our hospitals, every organization and agency of the churches should be kept aflame with the passion of New Testament evangelism. Our cities and towns and villages and country places are to echo continually with the sermons and songs of the gospel evangel. The people, high and low, rich and poor, the foreigners, all the people are to be faithfully told of Jesus and his great salvation, and entreated to come unto him to be saved by him and to become his fellow workers. The only sufficient solvent for all the questions in America—individual, social, economic, industrial, financial, political, educational, moral and religious—is to be found in the Saviourhood and Lordship of Jesus Christ.

> Give us a watchword for the hour,
> A thrilling word, a word of power;
> A battle cry, a flaming breath,
> That calls to conquest or to death;
> A word to rouse the church from rest,
> To heed its Master's high behest,
> The call is given, Ye hosts arise;
> Our watchword is Evangelize!
>
> The glad Evangel now proclaim,
> Through all the earth in Jesus' name,
> This word is ringing through the skies,
> Evangelize! Evangelize!
> To dying men, a fallen race,
> Make known the gift of Gospel Grace;
> The world that now in darkness lies,
> Evangelize! Evangelize!

A World Program

While thus caring for the homeland, we are at the same time to see to it that our program is coextensive with Christ's program for the whole world. The whole world is our field, nor may we, with impunity, dare to be indifferent to any section, however remote, not a whit less than that, and with our plans sweeping the whole earth, we are to go forth with believing faith and obedient service, to seek to bring all humanity, both near and far, to the faith and service of him who came to be the propitiation for our sins, and not for ours only, but also for the sins of the whole world.

His commission covers the whole world and reaches to every human being. Souls in China, and India, and Japan, and Europe, and Africa, and the islands of the sea, are as precious to him as souls in the United States. By the love we bear our Saviour, by the love we bear our fellows, by the greatness and preciousness of the trust committed to us, we are bound to take all the world upon our hearts and to consecrate our utmost strength to bring all humanity under the sway of Christ's redeeming love. Let us go to such task, saying with the immortal Wesley, "The world is my parish," and with him may we also be able to say, "And best of all, God is with us."

A Glorious Day

Glorious it is, my fellow Christians, to be living in such a day as this, if only we shall live as we ought to live. Irresistible is the conviction that the immediate future is packed with amazing possibilities. We can understand the cry of Rupert Brooke as he sailed from Gallipoli, "Now God be thanked who hath matched us with this hour!" The day of the reign of the common people is everywhere coming like the rising tides of the ocean. The people are everywhere breaking with feudalism. Autocracy is passing, whether it be civil or ecclesiastical. Democracy is the goal toward which all feet are traveling, whether in state or in church.

The demands upon us now are enough to make an archangel tremble. Themistocles had a way of saying that he could not sleep at night for thinking of Marathon. What was Marathon compared to a day like this? John C. Calhoun, long years ago, stood there and said to his fellow workers in the national Congress: "I beg you to lift up your eyes to the level of the conditions that now confront the American republic." Great as was that day spoken of by Mr Calhoun, it was as a tiny babe beside a giant compared to the day that now confronts you and me. Will we be alert to see our day and be faithful enough to measure up to its high demands?

The Price to be Paid

Are we willing to pay the price that must be paid to secure for humanity the blessings it needs to have? We say that we have seen God in the face of Jesus Christ, that we have been born again, that we are the true friends of Christ, and would make proof of our friendship for him by doing his will. Well, then, what manner of people ought we to be in all holy living and godliness? Surely we should be a holy people, remembering the apostolic characterization,

> Ye are a chosen generation; a royal priesthood, an holy nation, a peculiar people; that we should shew forth the praises of him who hath called you out of darkness into his marvelous light: which in time past were not a people, but are now the people of God.

Let us look again to the strange passion and power of the early Christians. They paid the price for spiritual power. Mark well this record: "And they overcame him by the blood of the Lamb, and by the word of their testimony; and they loved not their lives unto the death." O my fellow Christians, if we are to be in the true succession of the mighty days and deeds of the early Christian era, or of those mighty days and deeds of our Baptist ancestors in later days, then selfish ease must be utterly renounced for Christ and his cause and our every gift and grace and power utterly dominated by the dynamic of his cross. Standing here today in the shadow of our country's capitol, compassed about as we are with so great a cloud of witnesses, let us today renew our pledge to God, and to one another, that we will give our best to church and to state, to God and to humanity, by his grace and power, until we fall on the last sleep.

If in such spirit we will give ourselves to all the duties that await us, then we may go our ways, singing more vehemently than our forebears sang them, those lines of Whittier:

> Our fathers to their graves have gone,
> Their strife is passed, their triumphs won;
> But greater tasks await the race
> Which comes to take their honored place,
> A moral warfare with the crime
> And folly of an evil time.
>
> So let it be, in God's own sight,
> We gird us for the coming fight;
> And strong in Him whose cause is ours,
> In conflict with unholy powers,
> We grasp the weapons He has given,
> The light and truth and love of Heaven.

The Baptist Conception of Religious Liberty

E. Y. Mullins

[*Editorial note: See pages 6-7 for historical background of this sermon*].

Introduction

With Baptists, religious liberty is born of the direct vision of God. Sometimes it has been a dream when, like John Bunyan in the darkness of prison, they have gazed through the bars at the far–off stars. Sometimes it has been a theme of eloquent discourse when they have expounded it to others. Sometimes it has been a solace when they have gone into exile for conscience sake, and sometimes a battle cry when they have shed their blood for it. But always it has been a passion deep as life welling up from the depths of being in eternal faith and hope.

If I could express in a word the heroic spirit of Swedish Baptists seventy–five years ago, and after, I could tell you what religious liberty means. If I could give to you the distilled essence of the spirit of our Virginia fathers, and once more catch the vision of Roger Williams, of Rhode Island, who founded a commonwealth on the principle, I could set forth the truth. Nay, if I could reproduce in descriptive words the heroism of our brethren and sisters today in Russia, in Bessarabia, in Roumania, and many other countries, I would need no other words. It was expressed in immortal words in Oncken's reply to the Burgomaster: "Oncken," said he, when he had been arrested, "as long as I can lift my little finger I will put you down from preaching this gospel." "Mr. Burgomaster, as long as I can see God's mighty hand above your little finger I will preach this gospel."[1]

The Bases of Religious Liberty

Look then at the bases of religious liberty.

There are three great discoveries made by every human soul which grows normally to maturity. First, it discovers the world. To the babe the world is a part of itself. Even our own mothers are at first a mere patch of moving color and a soothing sound. But when the babe tries to pluck the flame of a candle and burns its hand, or bumps its head on the floor, it makes the first great discovery. It discovers that the world is different from itself. The self and the world become henceforth great realities. Later when the moral nature awakes the soul discovers God, the greatest of all realities. When a human soul discovers God, the foundation for religious liberty is laid.

People have wandered from the path of duty, civilization has gone astray, because these three realities, the self, the world, and God, have not been properly related. The human problem has been how to relate personality to society, the individual life to the corporate life. But how to relate the individual to God comes first. It is the key to all problems. The quest for economic liberty, intellectual liberty, civil liberty, all go back to religious liberty as the root.

Thomas Jefferson wrote his own epitaph before his death. It is most remarkable in the fact that, although he served as president of the United States eight years, there is no mention of that fact. The epitaph reads as follows: "Here lies buried Thomas Jefferson, Author of the declaration of American Independence—of the statute of Virginia for Religious Freedom, and Father of the University of Virginia." Jefferson had the spiritual vision to see that liberty is the fountainhead of civilization and that religious liberty is the mother of all other forms of liberty.

Sir Walter Besant, in his little book *Building the Empire*, shows a similar insight. In an early sentence he shocked my American sensibilities by the declaration that the British empire includes the British Isles, Australia, New Zealand, South Africa, Canada, and the United States of America. The reader is amazed until he reads further Sir Walter's statement that he is defining the empire not as a political or physical, but as a spiritual entity. He means that Great Britain was the seed plot of liberty for all these governments. The love of religious liberty is the deepest bond of unity and friendship among nations.

Religious liberty rests upon a person's original creation in God's image. The purpose of God in creation did not appear until the dust stood erect in the form of a human, as a free and self-determining being. A human being as a person created in God's image, free and spiritual, competent to deal directly with God, with an upward look, an endless discontent with the finite and temporal, a passionate yearning for the infinite and eternal; a human being, endowed with a conscience ringing in the soul like an alarm bell against wrong doing; a human being, with a will of one's own which one can misuse and bring on moral ruin, but which one can surrender to God; a human being, with an intellect hungering for infinite truth and eternally discontented; a human being, with a heart that no earthly object can satisfy; a human being, self-willed and sinful and then penitent and believing, redeemed by the power of Jesus Christ, Redeemer and Lord; a human being, recreated in the Divine image, with the witness of the Spirit in one's soul, telling of one's eternal destiny; a human being, as a child of God seeking to walk worthily of one's calling, and heir of all the ages—this is the being and these the endowments that demand that great boon we call religious liberty.

As Baptists understand it, religious liberty excludes certain things and implies certain other things. It implies certain rights and along with these involves certain duties and privileges. Let us look at these in order.

What Religious Liberty Excludes

First, religious liberty excludes a number of things. It excludes, for one thing, state authority in religion. The state depends on the use of force. Religion is moral and spiritual. The state uses coercion. Religion appeals only to freedom. The state deals with evil-doers. Religion seeks to produce righteous men and women. The state represses crime. Religion develops character.

Again, religious liberty excludes the principle of toleration in religion. To put the power and prestige of the state behind one form of religion and merely tolerate others is not religious liberty. It is religious coercion. God has not given the state any power to compel people in religion. Equal rights to all and special privileges to none is the true ideal. Some do not know the difference between toleration and liberty. If a snail could speak it would say to the tortoise "You go too fast for me." The clod would say to the snail: "You go so fast, you make me dizzy." But neither clod nor snail nor tortoise would know of the mighty flight of the eagle overhead. Religious toleration is the snail and tortoise. Religious liberty is the eagle.

Religious liberty excludes the right of the state to impose taxes for the support of one form of religion against the conscience of the people. All honor to the heroes of passive resistance who refuse to pay an obnoxious tax, which the state has no right to impose. A free church in a free state is the goal we should seek.

Again, religious liberty excludes the imposition of religious creeds by ecclesiastical authority. Confessions of faith by individuals or groups of Christians, voluntarily framed and set forth as containing the essentials of what they believe to be the gospel, are all right. They are merely one way of witnessing to the truth. But when they are laid upon consciences by ecclesiastical command, or by a form of human authority, they become a shadow between the soul and God, an intolerable yoke, an impertinence and a tyranny.

Religious liberty excludes centralized ecclesiastical government. Human beings, redeemed by Christ, regenerated by his Spirit, born of Divine power and grace, are capable of dealing directly with God. Each one has a right to a voice in religious affairs. God speaks directly to individuals. Even the humblest believer may be a channel of the highest divine wisdom. Democracy, or self-government in the church, is the New Testament ideal. All believers are entitled to equal privileges in the church.

Religious liberty excludes priestly mediators and sacramental power of salvation. We have one priest, Jesus Christ, our great High Priest. All believers are priests entering into the most Holy Place. God's grace flows freely and directly to all who have faith and respond to His call. God has not limited the gift of His grace to any particular human channel. No group has any monopoly of God's grace, to withhold or bestow it upon their own conditions. God's grace is direct. It is God's free gift. "Let us come boldly to the throne of grace," is the injunction of the sacred writer.

Religious liberty excludes infant baptism. Baptists refuse to treat the infant as a thing. We treat it as a potential person. We recognize its will, its intelligence, its freedom. We will not rob it of the joy of conscious obedience in baptism. Proxy faith is a counterfeit faith. The New Testament recognizes only personal faith. Train the growing child for God. Religiously we should do everything for the child, but nothing to it. Lead it to Christ. As the living flower at your feet requires the forces of the boundless universe to mould and shape it, so does the child require an infinite spiritual universe. As the flower needs the power of gravitation that grips all the systems, the sunlight that travels ninety-million miles to paint its petals, the mysterious and wondrous power of electricity, and the complicated water system of the planet, to mould and shape it, so also the child needs God's infinite truth, God's boundless love, God's immeasurable power and God's unspeakable grace to regenerate and mould the child into Christ's image. Religious liberty requires that we let the child, as it grows up, learn the truth for itself, repent and believe for itself, obey Christ for itself, be baptized for itself, rejoice and struggle and grow for itself. To deny it these things is to rob it of its religious rights.

What Religious Liberty Implies

Consider next what religious liberty implies. First of all, religious liberty implies the greatest of human rights. Let us glance at some of these rights.

The first is the right of direct access to God. No cloud, no shadow of human authority, should come between the soul and its God. The second is the individual's right to search for truth in religion. Jesus recognized this. He did not compel belief by Divine authority. He so lived and taught the truth that men and women discovered his messiahship for themselves. His revelations became their discoveries. Many things are revealed that people do not discover. The cause of many diseases was clearly revealed in signs and symptoms through the ages. But it required the genius and insight of a Pasteur to discover the germ. When he made this discovery he revolutionized the science of medicine. The facts of the solar system were revealed during all past ages. But not until Copernicus made his great discovery did we know that the sun is the center. Jesus was revealed to the disciples as the Divine Son of God, but not until by faith they discovered him did they understand him. "Who do ye say that I am?" was his question. "Thou are the Christ, the Son of the Living God," was their answer. He dawned upon them like a sunburst. They discovered his glory and were lifted to divine heights.

So also religious liberty implies the right of free utterance and propagation of truth. The evil powers of the world have ever sought to stifle people. Heroes have led the way in the witness for the truth. Martin Luther is one of the greatest heroes of all time because at a supreme moment in the spiritual history of the race, with every earthly power arrayed against him, at the Diet of Worms, he said: "Here I stand. I can do no otherwise. God help me."

Religious liberty implies the right of equal privilege in the church. There are no spiritual lords in the Christian religion, except the one Lord, Jesus Christ. Christ brings the common person to his or her rights. Under the old human systems, the church or state was everything, the common person nothing. The church or state was like the tree, enduring through the generations. Common folk were like the leaves on the tree that fell to the ground and perished with the seasons. The state or church was like the ocean, enduring through the centuries; common folk were like the waves, rising and falling and disappearing for ever. Christ says: "Let the common person speak. Give that one a voice in your affairs. Let God speak through her or him." Look at that group of worshipers in that first church at Corinth. All grades and classes in society are represented. There is a Greek with classic features indicating culture. There is a Roman, rugged and strong of feature. There is a rich person, and by the rich one's side a slave. There is a city official, and there is a regenerated outcast. There are the respectable and among them the scarlet-woman, washed and cleansed by the blood of Christ. There is a northern barbarian, and a swarthy Ethiopian; for Corinth was a cosmopolitan city representing the ends of the earth. The Roman government was an iron band holding the world together by force. Here is a new inward spiritual bond uniting all people on a new principle of common faith and hope and love. Here is loyalty and obedience to a common saviour, Jesus Christ, Who has shown them the way to God. Here is a new freedom, a new equality of privilege, a new fellowship. This Corinthian church is a new spiritual democracy. It is the seed plot of all future democracies, because it is an embodiment of religious liberty in its primary meaning of free access to God.

So also religious liberty implies the right of free association and organization for religious purposes. All people with religious beliefs and convictions have a right to organize and propagate their views. There never has been and never will be any human government, civil or ecclesiastical, with any right to curb or hinder or thwart the utmost freedom of people to associate themselves together, to organize, and to propagate the truth as they see it.

And this leads to the statement that religious liberty implies the right of human beings to demand of governments under which they live protection in the free exercise of their religion. That government that persecutes for religious beliefs commits a crime against God and humanity. That government that is partial in its treatment of religious beliefs violates the principles of common justice, transgresses eternal and inalienable human rights, and defies the will of God.

The Duties of Religious Liberty

Having considered the rights which religious liberty includes, I consider next what are the duties imposed. Among these duties are the following:

First of all is the duty to search for and discover truth. God gave us the Bible. God made the world. There is no conflict between truths. The city of truth that science is building up from the earth, when completed and purified, will be seen to be a suburb of the city of God, which is descending from heaven arrayed in the glory of a bride adorned for her husband. Let us not fear that God's revelation in nature will conflict with God's revelation in redemption. Christ is the key to both. Slowly science is fashioning a crown for him. Slowly economics and sociology are fashioning a crown for him. Slowly psychology and biology are fashioning a crown for him. Slowly his people are fashioning a crown for him. He Who went forth with a single crown will return crowned with many crowns. All the armies of truth shall follow him, and on his vesture shall be written his name: "King of Kings and Lord of Lords."

I name next the duty of sacrifice for truth. To discover truth is one thing. To be willing to sacrifice and even die for it is another. Christ's witnesses have ever been Christ's martyrs. Let us never forget:

> Though love repine and reason chafe,
> There comes a voice without reply,
> 'Tis man's perdition to be safe
> When for the truth he ought to die.

Let us also remember that

> By the light of burning martyrs Christ's bleeding feet I track,
> Toiling up new Calvaries ever, with the Cross that turns not back,
> And those mounts of anguish number how each generation learned
> Some new word in that grand credo which in prophet-hearts
> has burned
> Since the first man stood God-conquered with his face
> to heaven upturned.

A third duty is to protect with all our souls against religious oppression. Baptists believe in religious liberty for themselves. But they believe in it equally for all people. With them it is not only a right; it is also a passion. While we have no sympathy with atheism or agnosticism or materialism, we stand for the freedom of the atheists, agnostics and materialists in their religious or irreligious convictions. To God they stand or fall. They will render their account to the Eternal Judge, not to human beings. So also the Jew and the Catholic are entitled to protection in the exercise of their religious liberty. Baptists do not desire to share the errors of others, but we are, and ever have been, and ever will be passionate and devoted champions of the rights of all people. The supreme and inalienable right of all is the right to direct and free and unhindered approach to God.

The next duty involved in religious liberty is loyalty to the state. The state is ordained of God. It serves a Divine end and purpose. Baptists have ever been ardent patriots. Liberty is not license. Liberty is opportunity for service. Religious liberty is the prime condition for every kind of human progress. Let one have free access to God and hear God's voice, and that one will become a champion of law and order. That one will become a champion of the economic rights of all. That one will become an advocate of the golden rule in all industrial relations. That one will become an evangelist of sisterhood and brotherhood among the nations, of peace on earth and good will among them. That one will oppose war, knowing that war is directly opposed to the gospel of Christ. That one will pray for one's own country and for all countries. That one will live and strive and pray that one's own country may become a part of God's kingdom.

Finally, religious liberty involves the supreme duty of loyalty to Jesus Christ. Not license, self-will, or human will, but God's will as revealed in Christ is the goal of history and of religious liberty. There is no danger in this religious liberty centered and anchored in Jesus Christ. Catholics are afraid of it and want to impose the authority of the pope and the church. Cardinal Gibbons defines religious liberty as "the right to worship God according to the dictates of a right conscience, and practice that form of religion most in harmony with a person's duty to God." But a right conscience is a Catholic conscience, and the Catholic religion alone answers the above description as Cardinal Gibbons sees it. Wrapped up in that definition is all oppression. Gibbets and prisons and thumbscrews and racks are concealed in it. It can start martyr fires that would girdle the earth.

Another Catholic writer referring to the pope says:

> We acknowledge that authority; we proclaim it; we embrace it, as one surrounded by dark and turbulent waters clings to a lone spar lifting to safety above the perils of the deep. We may, indeed, hear the siren song of liberty; we may feel in our hearts the urge of our race to be free; we may be tempted to turn and walk no more in the way pointed out to us. But we know full well that liberty without authority is the kiss of death. As a kite without a string, a ship without a rudder, a meteor that has strayed from its orbit in the skies, so is a person when the tie that binds to the Creator is cut asunder. That person floats through life, a wayward and meaningless atom in the universe, with destiny thwarted and the future nothing but darkness, desolation and extinction. Oh, give us faith, that virtue which reaches down from heaven to lift the universe.

But authority here advocated is that of the pope and the Catholic church, and these are not the true authority. Jesus Christ is that authority. Unto him is committed the destinies of the human race. Let him have sway in human hearts and they will realize their true freedom. Freedom only comes when one finds one's true object and is impelled by a higher motive. No person finds the soul's true object until that one finds Jesus Christ. None have such spontaneity of action, such untrammeled energy and buoyancy as people who have acquired the freedom that Christ, the Son, gives. Look at Paul. He abounds in images that suggest spontaneity and exuberant joy. See him yonder when like a mighty swimmer rising above the billows of adversity and difficulty he exclaims, "I can do all things through Christ." Hear him as he spreads the wings of devotion, and in a splendid flight of mystic passion he shouts, "For me to live is Christ, and to die is gain." Observe him as he is caught in the mighty grip of moral enthusiasm and self-conquest, exulting in the joy of battle, "Thanks be to God, Who always leads me in victory through Christ." See him again as he is impelled onward, the embodiment of flaming love and quenchless hope and deathless ambition, running the Christian race as one who treads on air, and exclaiming, "Forgetting the things that are behind, I press towards the mark."

The moral career of Paul reminds one of the flight of some mighty eagle, long confined in a cage and then released. At first he is uncertain of his new feeling of freedom, but at length, becoming conscious of it, the heavy eyelids open, he looks about him, his dropping wings he gathers for flight, and then with a scream of joy he soars away to the clouds. His eagle soul has found its object, God's free air. Jesus Christ is the atmosphere of the soul. In him the soul finds its true object and freedom. Individuals become the slaves of Christ, because he makes them autonomous, sets them free.

Human history has seen the downfall of many false authorities in church and state. Crowns have been shattered and thrones sometimes broken down. But some have gathered the pieces of the broken thrones, and they are erecting another greater than all, and they are making of the shattered crowns another more glorious than all. On that throne they are placing Jesus Christ, and that glorious crown they are putting on his brow, and I can hear by the ear of faith the far away rising and falling of the mighty chorus of the nations:

> All hail the power of Jesus' name,
>   Let angels prostrate fall;
> Bring forth the royal diadem,
>   And crown Him, Lord of all.

Notes

[1] Editor's note. Johann Gerhard Oncken (1800—1884), the pioneer of the German Baptist movement in the nineteenth century, exercised a powerful voice for religious liberty, missions, education, and Baptist cooperative endeavors.

The American Baptist Bill of Rights

[*Editorial note: See pages 7-8 for historical background on this statement*].

A Pronouncement upon Religious Liberty

No issue in modern life is more urgent or more complicated than the relation of organized religion to organized society. The sudden rise of the European dictators to power has changed fundamentally the organic law of the governments through which they exercise sovereignty, and as a result, the institutions of religion are either suppressed or made subservient to the ambitious national programs of these new totalitarian states.

Four Theories of the Relation of Church and State.
There are four conceptions of the relation of church and state:

1. The church is above the state, a theory held by those who claim that their ecclesiastical head is the vicar of Christ on earth.
2. The church is alongside of the state, a theory held by the state churches of various countries.
3. The state is above the church, a theory held by the totalitarian governments.
4. The church is separate from the state, championed by the Baptists everywhere, and held by those governments that have written religious liberty into their fundamental laws.

Baptists Opened the Door of Religious Liberty

Three hundred years have passed since the establishment under Baptist leadership of the first civil government in which full religious liberty was granted to the citizens forming the compact. The original document preserved in the city hall, Providence, Rhode Island, is a covenant of citizens:

> We, whose names are hereunder, desirous to inhabit in the town of Providence, do promise to subject ourselves in active or passive obedience to all such orders or agreements as shall be made for public good for the body in an orderly way, by the major assent of the present inhabitants, masters of families, incorporated together into a town fellowship, and such others whom they shall admit unto themselves only in civil things.

These four concluding words opened wide the door to religious liberty.

Provided an Asylum for the Persecuted.
This document was written three hundred years ago by Roger Williams, a Baptist minister and a student under Lord Coke, who had been banished from the colony of Massachusetts for his espousal of the freedom of conscience. The founder of a civil commonwealth, called the Providence Plantations, he started a political movement that made the colony of Rhode Island the asylum of the persecuted and the home of the free.

Laid the Foundations of Religious Liberty.
The Baptists of England, through Leonard Busher, had in 1614 pleaded with James I for freedom of conscience. Roger Williams became the apostle of religious liberty in colonial America. Dr. John Clarke, the pastor of the Baptist church of Newport, Rhode Island, as agent of the Rhode Island Colony and Providence Plantations, secured from Charles II in 1663 a charter in which the religious liberty claimed by the colonists was guaranteed through a royal decree. For the first time in the history of the world a civil government was founded that guaranteed to its inhabitants absolute religious freedom.

Pleaded for the Religious Rights of All.
The Baptists of the colony of Virginia where between 1767 and 1778, forty-two Baptist ministers were jailed for preaching the gospel, through repeated memorials pleaded with the authorities for religious liberty. Favored by the leadership of Thomas Jefferson, James Madison, George Mason, John Leland, and other lovers of freedom, they secured the free

exercise of religion through the passage of the Bill of Rights in 1785. Not content with the winning of religious equality in Virginia, Baptists scrutinized the terms of the federal constitution and were largely instrumental in securing the passage of the First Amendment, which declares that "Congress shall make no law respecting an establishment of religion, or prohibiting the free exercise thereof." As to this, see the letter of George Washington to the Baptists of Virginia.

Religious liberty, as our Baptist ancestors defined it, was an emancipation from governmental and all other coercive restrictions that thwarted the free exercise of religion or their high purpose to achieve a Christlike character.

Baptists Stress Spirituality

The principles that animate the activities of the Baptists, principles that they hold to be clearly taught in the New Testament, are the worth of the individual; the necessity of the new birth; the preservation of Christian truth in Christian symbols; spirituality, or the free pursuit of Christian piety; the persuading of others through personal testimony, by the life of example, the preaching of the gospel, and the creation of Christian institutions to the end that the unbelieving will be reconciled to God through a personal faith in Jesus Christ; the organization of groups of obedient believers into churches of Christ, democratic in the processes and theocratic in the principles of their government, and the continued uplifting of human society through the spirit of Christ and the ideals of his kingdom, having as its final objective the establishment of the eternal, unchanging purpose of Almighty God in the hearts of humans and the institutions of humankind.

Affirm the Competency of the Human Soul in Religion.
The conception of the dignity of the individual, as held by Baptists, is grounded in the conviction that every soul possesses the capacity and the inalienable right to deal with God for one's self, and to deprive any soul of this right of direct access to God is to usurp the prerogatives of the individual and the function of God.

Free Churches Within a Free State.
Standing as we do for the principle of voluntariness in religion, grounded upon the competency of the human soul, Baptists are essentially

antagonistic to every form of religious coercion or persecution. We admit to our membership only those who give evidence that they are regenerated, but we recognize gladly that the grace of God is not limited to those who apply to us, but that our spiritual fellowship embraces all who have experienced the new birth and are walking in newness of life, by whatever name they may be called. We hold that the church of Christ, which in the Bible is called "the body of Christ," is not to be identified with any denomination or church that seeks to exercise ecclesiastical authority, but includes all the regenerated whoever and wherever they are, as these are led by the Holy Spirit. This church is a body without formal organization, and therefore cannot enter into contractual relations on any basis with the state. For this reason, Baptists believe in Free Churches within a Free State.

Today Baptists Feel Constrained to Declare Their Position

Since every session of the congress considers legislation that raises the question as to the relation of the federal government to the institutions and agencies of religion, and since recently many tendencies have appeared that involve the freedom of religion and conscience, and furthermore, since there are some state constitutions that do not have embodied in them the Bill of Rights of the federal constitution, Southern Baptists feel constrained to declare their position and their convictions.

The Trend Toward Paternalism.
Today the trend of government even in democratic countries, lies in the direction of greater centralization. The philanthropic activities of the churches within the United States are being taken over by the government. The defective, the indigent, and the dependent groups of our social order have long been supported from public funds. The greatest charity agent on earth today is our federal government. More and more the people are looking to the state to provide. As a nation we are becoming paternalistic. Efforts are now being made to place in the hands of the government the pensioning of those who are employed by the churches and the agencies that serve them; to grant to sectarian schools financial aid from tax-raised funds, and to support from public funds institutions that are established and managed by sectarian bodies.

Baptists Condemn the Union of Church and State.
Baptists hold that coercion of religious bodies through special taxes, the use of tax-raised funds for sectarian schools, and the appropriation of public money to institutions created to extend the power and influence of any religious body, violate the spirit of the First Amendment and result in the union of state and church.

Oppose Special Favors Extended to Any Ecclesiastical Body.
We oppose the establishing of diplomatic relations with any ecclesiastical body, the extension of special courtesies by our government to any ecclesiastical official as such, and the employment of any of the branches of our national defense in connection with religious services that are held to honor any ecclesiastical leader. All such violations of principle must be resisted in their beginnings.

Citizens of Two Commonwealths

We acknowledge ourselves to be citizens of two commonwealths, one earthly, the United States, the other heavenly, the Kingdom of God; and we claim the right to be good citizens of both. We recognize the sovereignty of the state and we give allegiance to the state, but we cannot give to the state the control of our consciences. We must obey God rather than humans.

The government resorts to coercion; we use persuasion. The government has authority over the acts of its citizens; we have to do with their motives. The business of the government is to make good laws; our business is to make good citizens, who continue to demand the enactment of better laws, embodying higher and still higher ethical standards. The end of governmental administration is equal justice under law. The end of our endeavor is the establishment of the will of God in the hearts and institutions of people. If one of us accepts an office in the government, that one recognizes it not only as a public trust, but also as a divine entrustment; for the powers that be are ordained of God. In a democracy like ours, it is possible to be a loyal American and a devoted Christian. This is true because religious liberty is an essential part of our fundamental law.

Defenders of Religious Liberty.
Believing religious liberty to be not only an inalienable human right, but indispensable to human welfare, Baptists must exercise themselves to the utmost in the maintenance of absolute religious liberty for their Jewish neighbors, their Catholic neighbors, their Protestant neighbors, and for everybody else. Profoundly convinced that any deprivation of this right is a wrong to be challenged, Baptists condemn every form of compulsion in religion or restraint of the free consideration of the claims of religion.

We stand for a civil state, "with full liberty in religious concernments."

>   W. O. Carver   W. T. Conner
>   Rufus W. Weaver   J. Clyde Turner
>   J. B. Lawrence   Theo. F. Adams
>   W. W. Hamilton

Religious Liberty
A Continuing Struggle

Brent Walker

Then God said, "Let us make humankind in our image, according to our likeness; and let them have dominion over the fish of the sea, and over the birds of the air, and over the cattle, and over all the wild animals of the earth, and over every creeping thing that creeps upon the earth." So God created humankind in his image, in the image of God he created them; male and female he created them. (Genesis 1:26–27)

Tell us, then, what you think. Is it lawful to pay taxes to the emperor, or not?" But Jesus, aware of their malice said, "Why are you putting me to the test, you hypocrites? Show me the coin used for the tax." And they brought him a denarius. Then he said to them, "Whose head is this, and whose title?" They answered, "The emperor's." Then he said to them, "Give therefore to the emperor the things that are the emperor's, and to God the things that are God's." (Matthew 22:17-21)

For freedom Christ has set us free. Stand firm, therefore, and do not submit again to a yoke of slavery. (Galatians 5:1)

The Biblical Roots of Freedom

"I will make them conform themselves, or I will harrie them out of the land."[1]

Who spoke these words? King James I of England—the man whose name appears on many of your Bibles. About whom was he speaking? They were seventeenth-century religious dissenters, ecclesiastical gadflies who objected to the oppressive state religion. They chafed under the heavy hand of the Anglican church and the English state that had merged a century earlier when King Henry VIII broke with Rome and declared himself to be at once king and head of the English church. These radical Christians believed in a seemingly novel, establishment-threatening idea of religious liberty that viewed the true church as separate from, and standing in judgment over, the civil state.

Religious liberty is well grounded in scripture. Its tap root runs deep into the creation accounts in Genesis. God's decision to "make humankind in His image" necessarily implies the freedom on our part to say yes or no—to choose for or against a relationship with God (Gen 1:27). Jesus foreshadowed the modern doctrine of the separation of church and state when he said, "Give therefore to the emperor the things that are the emperor's, and to God the things that are God's" (Matt 22:17). And who is not thrilled by the apostle Paul's bold declaration that: "For freedom Christ has set us free. Stand firm, therefore, and do not submit again to a yoke of slavery" (Gal 5:1).

Despite these biblical roots—or perhaps because of them—the idea of religious liberty was heady, dangerous stuff, or so thought King James. For centuries, the church and state had operated as something of a joint venture. Most thought society would come apart if the state did not support the church and the church did not prop up the state. Indeed, this understanding was made explicit in the Peace of Augsburg in 1555, which held that the people of a certain territory were required to adhere to the beliefs of the prince. King James, therefore, was bound and determined to stop the heresy of religious liberty by whatever means available.[2]

The Baptist Roots of Religious Freedom

To escape this kind of intolerance a young, rough and tumble Puritan preacher emigrated to Massachusetts Bay Colony in 1631. Roger Williams, called by some the "apostle of religious liberty," came preaching and teaching "soul freedom." Williams insisted that faith cannot be dictated by any civil or ecclesiastical authority, but must be nurtured freely and expressed directly to God without human interference. Picking up on Jesus' admonition about giving to the emperor and anticipating the American notion of church and state separation that would bear constitutional fruit a century–and–a–half later, Williams advocated a "hedge or wall of separation between the garden of the church and the wilderness of the world."[3]

Roger Williams was not bashful about speaking his mind. The Puritan theocrats in Massachusetts were no more amused at this kind of crazy talk than was King James. So they kicked Roger Williams out of the colony. He settled in what would become Rhode Island and founded a town he dubbed "Providence," because he believed that God had led him there. In Rhode Island Williams began what he liked to call the "livlie experiment" of religious liberty and founded the first Baptist church on North American soil.

Over the ensuing centuries, Baptists championed soul freedom and religious liberty with unrelenting vigor and asserted the absolute importance of the separation of church and state to protect that precious liberty. Isaac Backus, an eighteenth-century Congregationalist pastor and itinerant evangelist, developed Baptist sentiments and a keen appreciation for the need to assure religious liberty. In time he became "the most forceful and effective writer America produced on behalf of the pietistic or evangelical theory of the separation of church and state."[4] For Backus, religion was fundamentally a matter between God and human beings, not to be interfered with by the state. John Leland, thirty years younger than Backus, followed in Backus' footsteps, boldly advocating religious liberty and church-state separation. Leland was pastor of several churches in Virginia and preached far and wide. He also played a pivotal role in convincing James Madison, the author of the Constitution and the Bill of Rights, that the guarantees for religious liberty must be written down and made explicit in our foundational charter.

J. M. Dawson, the first executive director of the Baptist Joint Committee, once said, "If [historians] were to be asked who was most responsible for the American guaranty of religious liberty, their prompt reply would be 'James Madison'; but if James Madison might answer, he would as quickly reply, 'John Leland and the Baptists.' "[5]

Despite the urging of these and other Baptists, full-blown religious liberty was slow in coming—even in America. Centuries of religious intolerance were firmly ingrained and old habits died hard. All but four states (Rhode Island, Pennsylvania, Delaware, and New Jersey) had officially established churches and varying degrees of persecution and intolerance. All but two states (Virginia and Rhode Island) had religious qualifications for public office; five denied basic civil rights to Catholics; and in Vermont, blasphemy was a capital offense.[6]

But the wise founders of our republic had a different vision for the new country. They took the bold, radical step of separating church and state in civil society, much to the delight of Baptists like Backus and Leland. They provided in Article VI of the new Constitution that there would be no religious test for public office. Not only did the religion of the prince not bind the rest of the country, but the prince could not even be required to have a religion! These Baptist–inspired architects of the new nation decided that the federal government would not be permitted to make any law "respecting an establishment of religion, or prohibiting the free exercise thereof." These initial words of the Bill of Rights ensconced in the Constitution explicit protection for the freedom of religion and the doctrine of the separation of church and state. And, in time, these principles were applied to the states, as well as the federal government. One's status in the civil community simply would not depend on a willingness to espouse any religious confession.

The first of these religion clauses, the "establishment clause," has quite properly been interpreted to prevent government from promoting or endorsing religion or becoming unduly entangled in religious affairs. The second religion clause, the "free exercise clause," keeps government from impeding or burdening the exercise of religion. Both of these clauses, when taken together, require government to remain neutral toward religion—turning it loose, leaving it to flourish or flounder on its own. These religion clauses require government to accommodate religion without advancing it, protect religion without promoting it, lift burdens on the exercise of religion without extending religion an impermissible benefit.

For the first time in human history, a nation denied to itself the right to become involved in religious matters or violate the conscience of its citizens.

Current Threats to Religious Freedom

With a few lapses here and there over the past two centuries, our country has done a creditable job in preserving our rights of conscience and ensuring the separation of church and state—at least when compared with the track record of other nations. But, unfortunately, today this tradition is not universally accepted, even among those who call themselves Baptist. There are many who are threatened by unbridled soul freedom and religious liberty and who think the wall of separation between church and state is a modern secularist perversion. So our Baptist birthright weathers assaults from left and right; its preservation demands a continuing struggle.

The Baptist Joint Committee, now sixty years old and having survived recent attempts to undermine its work, continues to lead that struggle on behalf of millions of free and faithful Baptists. A quick look at four pressing church–state issues of the final decade of the twentieth century confirm that some Baptists have forgotten our heritage, and that we need to redouble our efforts to turn our heritage into a legacy.

*The Supreme Court Ruling of 1990 and
the Religious Freedom Restoration Act of 1993.*

In 1990, the United States Supreme Court ruled that religion is not entitled to any special constitutional protection against governmental regulation.[7] Five members of the court wrote that special protection for religious liberty is a "luxury" that we can no longer afford as a society. It took an act of Congress—the Religious Freedom Restoration Act of 1993 (RFRA)—to restore robust protections to the free exercise of religion. Although signed by a Baptist president and passed unanimously by the House of Representatives, three senators voted against its passage. Ironically, they were all Baptists—Robert Byrd (D–WV), Harlan Mathews (D–TN), and Jesse Helms (R–NC). Despite the adoption of RFRA—perhaps the most important piece of legislation affecting our religious liberties in our lifetime—some courts continue to apply its terms in ways unfriendly to religious freedom and entertain numerous challenges to its constitutionality. The Baptist Joint Committee, in coalition with other advocates of religious freedom, is working to defend RFRA in the courts, so that the act can fulfill its promise as a fundamental shield for our liberty.

Federal and State Aid to Parochial Schools.

Efforts continue unabated to give millions of federal and state tax dollars to parochial schools under the seductive rubric of "parental choice." Of course parents are entitled to choose private or parochial schooling for their children, but they are not entitled to "choose" the rest of the taxpayers to help them foot the bill. It would be unwise, unfair, and unconstitutional. Yet, many members of Congress who have advanced such proposals call themselves Baptist. Voucher schemes also have been proposed at the state level—in Wisconsin, Ohio, and Vermont. When the constitutionality of the Wisconsin plan was challenged, the Christian Life Commission of the Southern Baptist Convention filed a brief supporting its constitutionality. The Baptist Joint Committee stood firm opposing all of these voucher plans.

The New Welfare Bill and State Monies to Church Ministries.

Those who want to give tax dollars to parochial schools to teach religion have gone one step farther. In the new welfare law passed at the end of the one-hundred-and-fourth Congress, Senator John Ashcroft (R–MO) inserted a provision that would allow the states to give money directly to *churches* to help finance their ministries—with the blessing of many Baptists on the Hill. And, if the block grants are distributed in the form of vouchers, the money could be used to support religious worship and instruction. The Baptist Joint Committee opposed that scheme on constitutional grounds and to keep churches and religious organizations free from the governmental regulation that would inevitably accompany such government largesse. We still take seriously John Leland's admonition that "the fondness of magistrates to foster Christianity has done it more harm than all the persecutions ever did."[8] Elder Leland was right. The price tag of our valued freedom to pursue faithfully our ministry is the willingness to refuse offers of "help" from the magistrate.

Effort to Amend the Religion Clause in the Bill of Rights.

If all of this were not bad enough, the one-hundred-and-fourth Congress saw three proposals to amend the religion clauses in the Bill of Rights. These proposals would revolutionize our understanding of the proper relationship between religion and politics and tear down the wall of separation between church and state. One proposal, offered by Ernest Istook (R–OK), a former Baptist educated at Baylor University, would restore state–sponsored prayer to the public schools and state–endorsed speech in the public square. Another proposal, offered by Henry Hyde (R–IL) and modified by Dick Armey (R–TX), would result in similar types of state–sponsored religious exercises and speech. Even more problematic, the Hyde/Armey proposal extends religion equal "benefits," thus giving constitutional sanction to public funding of pervasively sectarian institutions and activities. Many Baptists, both in Congress and throughout the country, support these unfortunate proposals. For example, Richard Land, executive director of the Christian Life Commission of the Southern Baptist Convention, testified in favor of the Hyde/Armey proposal before the house subcommittee on the Constitution. The Baptist Joint Committee is leading a coalition of more than thirty-five religious, education, and civil liberties groups opposing *all* such proposals to amend the Constitution. In October 1995, we testified before the senate judiciary committee against the amendments.

These are but a few instances of the constant, pervasive, unremitting threats to our religious liberty. Roger Williams, Isaac Backus, John Leland: where are you today?

A Renewed Cry for the Baptist Heritage

It is time for us to teach our children and remind our adults about the great Baptist heritage of religious freedom and the separation of church and state. Let the clear cry be heard again. We believe in free souls. As Bill Moyers has said, we are all "grown ups before God" and competent to determine our own spiritual destinies. We believe in free churches. They must be autonomous and free to worship and practice their faith without governmental meddling and interference. We believe in a free state. The gears of church must never engage the gears of government to force the "god of the majority" on the consciences of the minority.

We all say that we want freedom, but talk is easy and cheap. Choosing is scary, and deciding is frightening. It is tough to make hard choices, to live in a climate of moral ambiguity, to tolerate religious differences in a free state—opinions that fly in the face of all that we believe and hold dear. And sometimes many Baptists no less than others are willing to surrender their liberty in exchange for the temporary security and comfort that conformity brings.

In his letter to the Galatians, Paul was dealing with those in his day who were trying to escape from freedom: Christians who were trying to crawl back under the security blanket of certainty. But the apostle sounds a clarion call to those Galatians who, as the Judiazers urged, shirked the freedom of Christ's gospel and lusted after the predictability and comfort of the law. But Paul calls it nothing less than slavery.

It is my prayer and the focus of the ministry of the Baptist Joint Committee that we not forget our heritage. We must remember our forbears like Roger Williams, Isaac Backus, and John Leland—and the principles of soul freedom, religious liberty, and church–state separation that they and others worked so tirelessly to advance. Then once again we will be able to say with the apostle Paul, "Stand firm, therefore, and do not submit again to a yoke of slavery," and really mean it.

Notes

[1] John A. Armstrong, "Restless for Religious Liberty," *Report from the Capital* 44/5 (May 1989): 4.

[2] Ibid.

[3] Edwin S. Gaustad, *Liberty of Conscience: Roger Williams in America* (Grand Rapids: Wm. B. Eerdmans, 1991) 207.

[4] William G. McLoughlin, *Isaac Backus on Church, State, and Calvinism: Pamphlets, 1754–1789* (Cambridge: Harvard University Press, 1968) 1.

[5] J. M. Dawson, *Baptists and the American Republic* (Nashville: Broadman Press, 1956) 117.

[6] Douglas Laycock, " 'Nonpreferential aid' to Religion: A False Claim About Original Intent," *Wm. & Mary Law Review 27 (1986): 875, 916.*

[7] *Employment Division v Smith*, 494 U.S. 872 (1990).

[8] L. F. Greene, ed. *The Writings of the Late Elder John Leland* (New York: Arno Press, 1969) 278.

Praying in Public

Michael Bledsoe

Beware of practicing your piety before others in order to be seen by them; for then you have no reward from your Father in heaven. (Matthew 6:1)

And whenever you pray, do not be like the hypocrites; for they love to stand and pray in the synagogues and at the street corners, so that they may be seen by others. Truly I tell you, they have received their reward. But whenever you pray, go into your room and shut the door and pray to your Father who is in secret; and your Father who sees in secret will reward you. (Matthew 6: 5-7)

[*Michael Bledsoe preached this sermon on 15 January 1995, at the Riverside Baptist Church in Washington DC, where he is the pastor. Bledsoe's affection for his congregation—what he calls "our beloved, little church"—is obvious*].

The Appearance of Faith

Listen to this advice printed in a document given especially to those who govern. When this advice became public, it created quite a stir because it confirmed what some people had suspected all along about their leaders.

> Every one admits how praiseworthy it is [in a person who governs] that they keep faith, and [live] with integrity and not with craft. Nevertheless our experience has been that [those who govern] who have done great things have held good faith of little account . . . and in the end have overcome those who have relied on their word.[1]

And listen carefully to this passage because it has special significance for the topic of this sermon.

> It is unnecessary for [a person who governs] to have all good qualities . . . but it is very necessary to appear to have them. And I shall dare to say this also, that to have them and always observe them is injurious, and that to appear to have them is useful; to appear merciful, faithful, humane, religious, . . . There is nothing more necessary to appear to have than this last quality, inasmuch as people judge generally more by the eye than by the hand.[2]

This document was not written in this decade to American politicians. It was written by Machiavelli more than four hundred years ago and was entitled, *The Prince*.

While I am not positive, I believe that it was Walter Lippman who once said something to the effect that there can be no liberty for a community that lacks the means by which to detect lies. The historic Baptist commitment to liberty is a commitment to telling the truth, and it is not coincidental that such truth-telling took its turn pointing into the face of an intrusive state. Perhaps all of us would be well served by a careful reading of Machiavelli's advice to princes. For we see that a certain duplicity has existed among the powerful for centuries. And as Machiavelli noted, the religious issue plays especially well among the people. What was one of the first, if not the first, agenda items mentioned by the self-proclaimed revolutionary congress of the United States in 1994? That an amendment would be offered to "put prayer back" in school!

The irony of this was eloquently stated by the professor of history, Garry Wills, in an Op-Ed piece in the Washington Post. Wills noted that the new congress opened its session with prayer. Wills wrote, "Republicans think our schools have failed because they have given up prayer, yet also believe that Congress has been little better than a cesspool in recent years, and all that time its members have been praying constantly."[3]

This issue of prayer in public schools is not only a Republican idea, however. For in fact the three Democratic candidates in the DC mayoral elections of 1994 endorsed the idea of prayer in school.

A Cut Flower Civilization

Why this urgency about praying in public schools? How is it that many of our Baptist brothers and sisters and colleagues have called for this amendment? The executive director of the Baptist Joint Committee on Public Affairs (this is Baptists' watchdog agency on religious liberty), James Dunn, eloquently stated it when he briefed editors in October of 1994. "Four decades ago," Dunn said, "Harvard professor Pitirim Sorokin called America a 'Cut flower civilization,' saying that we still had the bloom of some moral values in our public and private life but had cut off the roots with the withering of religious experience and commitment." "Now," Dunn asserted, "we are living in the *Day of the Dead Flowers*."[4]

The Day of Dead Flowers! Maybe this explains why the Democratic mayoral candidates in DC, all African-American, recently endorsed the idea of public school prayer. They are not, as the black scholar Stephen L. Carter noted in *The New Yorker*, "dupes of the religious right," but they live in a city "where the murder rate exceeds that of Northern Ireland."[5] Dunn's insight is accurate for understanding why there is such support for prayer in school among many African-American clergy. To use Stephen Carter's words, those mayoral candidates and others like them represent "the voice of a community crying out desperately for a stable set of values to pass on to the next generation, which is seriously at risk."[6] Unlike liberal whites who have for the most part given up on prayer as anything but an exercise in futility, black Christians tend not to be moral relativists. Which is to say, they still believe in prayer. Hence, we have both Republicans and Democrats who are poised to put *public praying* back in public schools.

Historically Baptists have opposed such an amendment. Has the time come to change that position? I will argue that it has *not* and that in these dangerous times and for the sake of religious liberty, it is especially important that we resist this temptation.

Jesus' Perspective on Prayer

Where do we begin in trying to understand this issue? Can we not agree, whether we wear the label of liberal or conservative, Republican or Democrat, that we begin with Jesus' words about prayer? I think it not only logical but mandatory that we begin there. Listen again to Jesus' powerful words on prayer from the Sermon on the Mount as paraphrased by Clarence Jordan:

> See to it that your effort to do right is not based on a desire to be popular. If it is, you"ll get no help from your spiritual Father. . . .
> And when you pray, don't be like the phonies. For they love to stand up and pray in church and at public occasions, so they might build a reputation as pray-ers. The truth is, that's all they'll get out of it. But you, when you pray, go to your bedroom, shut the door, and pray to your Father in private. And your Father, who sees the inner life, will respond to you. (Matt 6:1,5-6, *The Cotton Patch Version*)

Is it not safe to say that if there was one thing in particular that Jesus detested it was the parading of religious piety in public? His instruction to us is that prayer is to be private. When Pat Robertson and his cabal pray on television, when Jerry Falwell and other tele-evangelists pray, do they pray in the public square? No, my friends, they stand not upon one street corner and pray but they pray on tens of thousands of street corners at the same time, praying in public and seen by the world. We have it on good authority--the authority of Jesus himself--that they have received their reward.

But some might ask, didn't Jesus pray in public? Jesus' prayers took place privately when he went off alone into some quiet space or in the assembly of the faithful, that is, he prayed in the synagogue and at worship. This fact should not escape our attention.

There are some who would suggest that the Hebrew scriptures would defend the idea of public prayer in public schools. Often they cite 2 Chronicles 7:14, "If my people who are called by my name humble themselves, and pray and seek my face, and turn from their wicked ways, then I will hear from heaven, and will forgive their sin and heal their land."

This is a wonderful scripture. The irony, however, is that people who claim to love the scriptures often do such a shoddy job of reading them! This passage is part of a larger passage dealing with the dedication of the temple. For more than one chapter we have Solomon praying *in the temple* that God would attend to the prayers of the people who pray there. God then appeared to Solomon in the night and told him that his prayer was heard. The passage quoted, "If my people who are called by my name," is part of God's answer to Solomon's prayer **in** the temple.

But ask yourself a more provocative question. Who told us that God embraces this, our, particular nation state? Who are these *"people called by my name?"* They are the covenant people of Israel, a name given to the chosen people who struggled with God. This is not an instruction given to simply any nation state. Of course, people across the earth and throughout the ages have confused God with their own nation. Do you recall the dictator of Iraq, Saddam Hussein, praying in public during the Gulf War? Most nations and their leaders want God on their side in time of war. But God is God of all the nations, not any one nation in particular, including the United States. The instruction in 2 Chronicles is given to the covenant people as an affirmation of their prayers in the temple.

You will note as well that there is no instruction given by Jesus about prayer helping to sustain the Roman empire or the culture of his time. By the way, did you know that the Romans considered Christians to be atheists? They concluded this because Christians would not pray in public the Roman prayers to the Roman gods. Thus they were martyred by the tens of thousands.

The biblical record and Jesus' words are clear on this matter: prayer is to be done in private or in the worshiping community with humility.

The Nation State and Values

But what about this important issue of passing along stable values to our children? How can we do that and seek God's blessing and protection of the land we live in and love?

Some continue to insist that the rising rates of teen pregnancy, youth violence, and drug use have increased rapidly in the years since public school-led prayer was banned. Stephen Carter responds by saying, "This is reminiscent of the charming but statistically naive point somebody came up with years ago: television viewership and lung cancer were both increasing, so one must cause the other." There is, as Carter points out, "no reliable data that more prayer in public schools would lead to more morally upstanding children."[7]

In point of fact, what were they praying for in the days of slavery? What were they praying for in the days of segregation and gender apartheid? If one wishes to see how diabolical the mixing of religion and government can be, one need only look at European history, which is bathed in the blood of religious wars. The question of values is tricky, and we must ask ourselves, what values would the state like to impart to our children through their state-led prayers? And this is precisely where my appeal lies with regard to my African-American colleagues who support a prayer amendment: *we dare not trust a racist nation nor a government with a racist history to fashion a prayer for our children.* We might get values, but they are liable to be counter to everything we cherish about the gospel of freedom and justice.

That said, I still believe in the efficacy of prayer and believe with all my heart that children and *especially adults* stand in the need of prayer.

Praying in Public

Such a belief should lead us beyond a simplistic opposition to public prayer in public schools. By that I mean that we cannot be satisfied with smugly saying we believe in the separation of church and state. We must take seriously these two indisputable points: prayer is good for the soul, and our children and nation are at risk. Prior to offering a solution to this problem, permit one technical point.

When the Supreme Court ruled on prayer, it ruled on the publicly led prayer in school. It did not, as often argued, throw God out of the classroom nor prayer out of school! Every child has the right to pray any time they wish in school. And Jesus' instruction on private prayer is helpful here. Our children should know they can pray within the sacred space of their spirits.

Do you recall Jesus' parables of yeast? Listen to this parable of our Master. "The Kingdom of Heaven is like yeast which a woman took and mixed in three measures of flower until it was all leavened" (Matt 13:33). Have you held yeast in your hand? It is small. Have you cooked with it and watched it as it bubbled and then, placed within the dough, raised that dough? Have you smelled its aroma, filling a house with its delicious scent? Such is prayer.

We can claim with hope and courage that beautiful promise contained in 2 Chronicles: God will attend to our prayers and through God's people, the land can be healed. Your prayers are like yeast, leavening the loaf. And I ask you, is not this our beloved, little church like that yeast?

We have people working throughout several layers in our society. From Capitol Hill to the Executive Office building, from the Department of Justice to the IRS, from the counseling rooms of lawyers to the counseling rooms of doctors, from nursing homes to school rooms, we have people who are living lives of faith and hope and love. We pray collectively here in worship, and we pray individually, asking God to hear the prayers of His people on behalf of the land we love.

Martin Luther King, Jr., often referred to the people of God as "the beloved community." This is what we attempt to create in this local church. You will note that Riverside--like so many churches, synagogues and mosques--is located next to schools, residences, and government buildings. We pass values along to our culture, and we do our best to invite people here to pray with us, even as we pray for them and ourselves.

So let us continue resisting the state intruding into the realm of religion and religion from intruding into the realm of the state. That does not mean we do not converse! Far from it. We speak clearly and loudly to our fellow citizens and our leaders to let justice roll down like waters and righteousness like a mighty stream.

I commend you, Riverside, for taking the necessary step of inviting young people into our church. This is, it seems to me, the way to go about countering the moral chaos around us. Interestingly, I received a phone call not long ago from a well-meaning individual affiliated with a South West community group who wanted to know if our after-school program would be interested in receiving a donation of one hundred dollars. Of course, I said yes. But this person went on to tell me that one of their members had visited an after-school program in another church and shared their concern that too much time seemed to be spent on religious instruction in those programs. This is just as confused as the right-wing views on imposing prayer on public schools.

I'm not interested in white, liberal guilt that tries to soothe its conscience by donating money but then wants to tell a church it should not be teaching "religion." I can assure you that if a program gets set up in this church, it will deal with prayer and things religious. If that is offensive, then take the hundred dollars and start your own after-school program that tries to instill values in our young people. And good luck! We don't want the state's money because the state just might think it should tell us how to pray—and that is also the same reason we do not need public praying in school.

I would suggest as well that the government leaders who think prayer is important take time to pray. For the truth is, there is absolutely nothing standing in the way for a leader to lead in prayer with young people. They can show up before or after school in any number of churches, synagogues, or mosques and lead children in prayer who want to be so led.

Allow me to conclude with a prayer from one of the finest and best Christian men who ever walked this earth. Walter Rauschenbusch was a pioneering Baptist preacher who, in the nineteenth century, became concerned about the social conditions around him. His prayer is worth our hearing and worthy of our lips.

> O God, we pray thee for those who come after us, for our children, and the children of our friends, and for all the young lives that are marching up from the gates of birth, pure and eager, with the morning sunshine on their faces. We remember with a pang that these will live in the world we are making for them. We are wasting the resources of the earth in our headlong greed, and they will suffer want. We are building sunless houses and joyless cities for our profit, and they must dwell therein. We are making the burden heavy and the pace of work pitiless, and they will fall wan and sobbing by the wayside. We are poisoning the air of our land by our lies and our uncleanness, and they will breathe it. . . .
>
> Help us to break the ancient force of evil by a holy and steadfast will and to endow our children with purer blood and nobler thoughts. Grant us grace to leave the earth fairer than we found it; to build upon it cities of God in which the cry of needless pain shall cease; and to put the yoke of Christ upon our business life that it may serve and not destroy. . . .
>
> Grant us a vision of the far off years as they may be if redeemed by the children of God, that we may take heart and do battle for thy children and ours.[8]

Amen.

Notes

[1]Nicolo Machiavelli, *The Prince,* trans. W. K. Marriott (New York: Alfred A. Knopf, 1992) 79.

[2]Ibid., 80-81.

[3]Garry Wills, "Newting the Constitution," *The Washington Post*, 8 January 1995, C1-2.

[4]James M. Dunn made these remarks in an oral presentation before the executive board of The Baptist Joint Committee on Public Affairs at the Riverside Baptist Church, Washington DC, 3 October 1995.

[5]For an incisive analysis, see the entire article in Stephen Carter, "Let Us Pray," *The New Yorker*, 5 December 1994, 64-67.

[6]Ibid., 64.

[7]Ibid., 67.

[8]Winthrop Hudson, *Walter Rauschenbusch. Selected Writings* (New York: Paulist Press, 1984) 229.

The Kind of Prayer That Honors God and That God Honors

Stan Hastey

> And whenever you pray, do not be like the hypocrites; for they love to stand and pray in the synagogues and at the street corners, so that they may be seen by others. Truly I tell you, they have received their reward. But whenever you pray, go into your room and shut the door and pray to your Father who is in secret; your Father who sees in secret will reward you.
> (Matthew 5:5-6)

Some sermons are easier to prepare and preach than others.

When asked to contribute a sermon to this collection on religious freedom, I was pleased to say, "Yes." After nearly a quarter century of writing, lecturing, and preaching about what William Lee Miller calls our nation's "first liberty," I figured this was a task I could fulfill with relative ease.

Then came the letter with more specific instructions, and, as the saying goes in Washington, "It's all in the fine print." The fine print in that letter asked that I contribute a sermon on prayer, specifically on prayer in public schools.

So I recommitted myself to the project, thinking I could pull some thoughts together, thoughts I've heard and borrowed over the years on what is admittedly one of the most persistently misunderstood and therefore most disagreed-upon subjects in the public arena during our lifetimes.

Then came the hard part. This was not to be a lecture on the relative merits and demerits of religious exercises in the schools. After all, the reader wanting that kind of treatment of the subject could consult dozens of books and articles written by experts far more qualified than I.

"This is to be a sermon," I kept telling myself, "and a sermon is not a lecture or a treatise. What can I possibly say about prayer in public schools in a sermon? What could I possibly say in a sermon on the subject that might enlighten or even move a reader or hearer?"

As if those questions were not daunting enough, another layer of uncertainty crowded its way into my consciousness as well. That uncertainty has to do with my own sense of inadequacy in the art of praying.

So what I find myself having to confess from the outset is that for me, more often than not, prayer does not come easily. More often than not, not even private prayer is easy for me, let alone the public variety. Then I remembered what Jesus had to say about prayer in his sermon from the mountain as recorded in Matthew's account of the gospel.

Assuming Matthew's placement of this inspired discourse at the very beginning of Jesus' ministry is correct, we can in turn assume that what Jesus set forth that day was something of a self-conscious effort to summarize what it was God had sent him to say and do. In the parlance of secular politics, we might say the sermon from the mountain was Jesus' platform.

Tucked away about halfway through that great sermon is the summary of what Jesus believed about prayer. But this is more than what Jesus *believed* about prayer; it is what Jesus knew about prayer from his own intimate communion with the God who had sent him on his mission.

You will note the saying on prayer follows immediately on the heels of a similar warning:

> Beware of practicing your piety before others in order to be seen by them. . . . So whenever you give alms, do not sound a trumpet before you, as the hypocrites do in the synagogues and in the streets, so that they may be praised by others. . . . But when you give alms, do not let your left hand know what your right hand is doing, so that your alms may be done in secret." (Matt 6:1-4)

The parallelism is almost absolute in the two sayings, first concerning the right way to present one's offering, then the right way to pray.

Yet there is more—far more—to the teaching. For Jesus went on to lay down a model of how prayer ought to be offered in the spirit he had just advocated, presumably in the privacy of one's own room, out of the sight of others, a prayer between the needy soul and that soul's merciful God.

But there's still more. Following the giving of the model prayer, Jesus added a third stanza to the warnings against public almsgiving and public prayer, this one having to do with public fasting.

> And whenever you fast, do not look dismal, like the hypocrites, for they disfigure their faces so as to show others that they are fasting. . . . But when you fast, put oil on your head and wash your face, so that your fasting may not be seen by others but by your Father who is in secret." (Matt 6:16-18)

So there we have it. The sum of the matter is unmistakably this: Jesus didn't think much of the public parading of one's piety when the motive of piety's expression was to impress others.

Having confessed my own profound sense of inadequacy in the practice of prayer, let me now add a second disclaimer, this one about not judging others. Jesus had a profound, or better yet, a unique ability to see through hypocrisy. So he could legitimately issue such warnings against the hypocrisies of almsgiving, praying, and fasting he observed all about him in the false piety of the day.

But when I begin to make judgments about the motives of those I observe practicing their piety, even in public, I need to say that I do so with considerable trepidation. Not all public prayer is hypocritical or, if it is, then we should stop praying in church. Praying in church, by the way, may be even harder than preaching in church. At least, I find it so. For what can be more presumptuous than the presumption of praying in behalf of others?

All of this brings me at last to the matter of public prayer in public schools, a practice I've opposed for as long as I can remember thinking about it. Here's why.

More important than the arguments against public prayer in public schools based on the constitution of the United States or any other public policy consideration is the theological truth that the prayer that is worth anything at all is the kind of prayer that honors God and that God honors.

Above I alluded to the almost presumptuous nature of public prayers in church. If there is any truth to that notion at all, then how much more presumptuous is it for an agent of the secular state to presume to pray over the captive audience in a public school classroom?

And what, after all, is the purpose of such prayer? Some have argued that no higher motivation need be cited than that of bringing a little peace and quiet to the classroom at the beginning of the school day. But is that, theologically speaking, a sufficient reason?

Some have argued that if the houses of Congress and the U.S. Supreme Court begin their work days with public prayers, why deprive schoolchildren of the privilege? Theologically speaking, I would counter by asking another question. Why do, and why should, the Congress and Supreme Court offer public prayers?

First as a reporter and later as a news analyst in the nation's capital, I've heard many such prayers and always wondered whether they are the kind of prayers that truly honor God and that God really honors. I'm not so sure, to be absolutely candid, because such prayers often seem to me to be offered as something akin to a good luck charm. So often they sound like prayers offered to some generic god who is somehow expected to respond in a kind of generic way to whatever such bodies happen to be doing on a given day.

Worse still, at times I've heard such prayers offered in such a way as nearly to presume that God somehow owes something back in exchange for such public piety. This is what I've called the "God-as-national-mascot" syndrome. It is a kind of tit-for-tat approach to prayer in which God is expected to be our tribal deity in exchange for our public professions of piety.

The ancient prophets of Israel had a lot to say about this kind of piety and prayer. Or more precisely, Israel's prophets reported that God had something to say about such public displays of piety. Amos, for example, put Yahweh's words thus:

> I hate, I despise your festivals,
>   and I take no delight in your
>   solemn assemblies.
> Even though you offer me your
>   burnt offerings and grain offerings,
> I will not accept them;
> and the offerings of well-being of
>   your fatted animals
> I will not look upon.
>
> Take away from me
>   the noise of your songs;

> I will not listen to
> the melody of your harps.
>
> But let justice roll down
> like waters,
> and righteousness
> like an overflowing stream. (Amos 5:21-24)

More recently, a modern-day prophet named Justo González said very much the same thing with reference to the subject of public prayers in public schools. He noted that many of those politicians in Washington and elsewhere who espouse such prayers also oppose bilingual education in schools and civil rights laws. Furthermore, he noted, these same politicians also advocate budget cuts in social programs and tough anti immigrant legislation. González goes on to say:

> Thus the same political tendency that shows a significant lack of regard for the demands for justice of the biblical God urges prayer in school. Why? Certainly not because such prayer will make us a more just society—that does not seem to be a main concern of those who campaign for prayer in schools. Rather, the function of prayer in school would be to sacralize the order of what are still segregated schools—and have become even more so in recent years. This "God" to whom prayer will be addressed will not be the defender of the alien and the poor but rather the defender of our borders against "aliens"—who in scripture have God's protection—and of the dominant culture against the inroads of minorities. This "God" is not the God of Scripture. It is a pagan god, and just as much an idol as were Baal and his cohorts.[1]

What I suspect is that much of the public parading of piety in places like Washington falls under the same judgment. So theologically speaking, I find it terribly hard to make a case for public prayers in public schools from the argument that if the adults in Congress and the Supreme Court do it, then surely a little public prayer in the public schools wouldn't hurt anyone.

Some express shock and even horror that a Baptist, of all people, would express such an opinion. Yet as a Baptist who has done some digging around in the history of the Baptist movement, I'm a bit shocked at our abysmal ignorance of who our ancestors were and what they believed about such matters.

Thomas Helwys, one of our earliest English ancestors, for example, in the year 1612 was sent off to Newgate Prison in London for sending King James an autographed copy of a treatise he had written concerning false religion.

Apparently Helwys had made an effort to present the king with a copy of his work, titled *A Short Declaration of the Mistery of Iniquity*, only to be rebuffed. So he did the next best thing. He wrote King James a note on the flyleaf of the copy he sent him. His words, so piercing then, are still so today:

> Heare O King, and dispise not ye counsell of ye poore, and let their complaints come before thee. The King is a mortall man, and not God therefore hath no power over ye immortall soules of his subjects, to make lawes and ordinances for them, and to set spirituall Lords over them. If the King have authority to make spirituall Lords and lawes, then he is an immortal God and not mortall man. O King be not seduced by deceivers to sin so against God Whom thou oughtest to obey, nor against thy poore subjects. . . . God save ye King.[2]

For his impertinence, Helwys rotted in prison for the better of four years before dying there in 1616.

Now one of the theological problems I have with the practice of public prayer in public schools is that no one has yet figured out a way for such prayers to be said without putting some public official, to paraphrase Thomas Helwys, in charge of the immortal souls of children who are in school because the state requires them to be there.

That is why, back in 1982 during the white-heat stage of the last big debate in the U.S. senate over a proposed constitutional amendment on school prayer, the attorney general of the United States was forced to acknowledge in a press release that if the amendment were passed some public official would have to write the prayer to be recited. The simple fact is that no one has yet to figure out how it would not be so.

So what's wrong with public prayers in public schools?

From the standpoint of the constitution of the United States, there's plenty wrong with such prayers. From the vantage point of public policy, there's a lot wrong with them.

But from the Christian perspective, what's most wrong with public prayers in public schools is much more basic than constitutional and public policy arguments. For that which is fundamentally wrong with public prayers in public schools is what always has been wrong with public piety—its natural tendency to be more hypocritical than genuinely pious.

"Beware of practicing your piety before others in order to be seen by them" (Matt 6:1), Jesus warned.

"But whenever you pray, go into your room and shut the door and pray to your Father who is in secret" (Matt.6:6).

Only when we pray in that spirit will we be offering the kind of prayer that honors God and that God honors.

Notes

[1] Justo L. Gonzalez, *Manana: Christian Theology from a Hispanic Perspective* (Nashville: Abingdon Press, 1990) 98.

[2] As cited in H. Leon McBeth, *The Baptist Heritage: Four Centuries of Baptist Witness* (Nashville: Broadman Press, 1987) 103-104.

Civil Religion
and Religious Liberty

Derek H. Davis

Then Jesus said to the Jews who had believed in him, "If you continue in my word, you are truly my disciple; and you will know the truth, and the truth will make you free."
(John 8:31-32)

Civil religion is "a perversion of true religion." Civil religion is nothing more than "counterfeit infidelity." Civil religion is, in fact, "state-funded support of religion."[1] With these stern descriptions, Jim Spivey, professor at Southwestern Baptist Seminary, warns of the dangers of civil religion.

Senator Mark Hatfield seconded the motion at a national prayer breakfast in 1973. Hatfield described civil religion as "faith . . . in a small and exclusive deity, a loyal spiritual Advisor to power and prestige, a Defender of only the American nation, the object of a national folk religion devoid of moral content."[2]

And Welton Gaddy affirms these perspectives when he calls civil religion "an unholy marriage of religious and political thought" whose confessors "tend to equate God and country, wrap the Bible in the flag," and see "no conflict between it and religious faith."[3]

Just what is this beast called civil religion that is the target of Spivey, Hatfield, and Gaddy? By most accounts, civil religion is a form of religion that gives sacred meaning to national life. It is a kind of theological glue that holds a nation together by binding it simultaneously to the dimensions of the transcendent. Civil religion is a way for Americans to recognize the sovereignty of God over their nation without getting bogged down in theological differences. Some sociologists even claim that some kind of civil religion is indispensable for the maintenance of the social order. But is it intrinsically idolatrous, immoral, and anti-Christian? I wish to suggest that civil religion, properly understood, is none of these things, but that it actually flows quite naturally out of distinctive Baptist views on religious liberty. In short, if we understand the term "civil religion" correctly, it just might be okay for Baptists to be advocates of civil religion.

Now Baptists have always been concerned about religious liberty, not just for themselves, but for others as well. They have always been most interested in the kind of religious liberty that permits each and every human being to serve the dictates of his or her own conscience. Roger Williams did not found Rhode Island to give the Baptists a colony to rival Puritan Massachusetts or Anglican Virginia but to act upon his vision of religious liberty. Williams believed that the best way to secure religious liberty for everyone was to separate church and state, to divide civil authority from spiritual matters. Roger Williams, not the religiously unorthodox Thomas Jefferson, coined the image of the "wall of separation" in 1644, a metaphor that today is praised by those who approve of the way church-state relations has evolved in our nation, but cursed by those who do not.

Is the separation of church and state a Baptist distinctive? Yes, as surely as the change of the weather in Texas. Is it an exclusively Baptist position? Not at all. The fact is that church-state separation is for some grounded in their theology, yet it stands as a political principle shared with many persons of other faiths and even with many of no faith at all.

Jimmy Carter was right, but it seems didn't know how right, when he said: "If there's one thing about Baptists that sets us aside from any other denomination, it's our total and complete commitment to the separation of church and state."[4] Carter spoke accurately, but in an ironic way. Some assume, as it seems Carter did, that church-state separation is one of the best of foundational political principles upon which our nation has been built. What this quotation shows, however, is that for Carter, church-state separation is not merely a political principle; it is a political principle grounded in his religious identity.

While many in our nation affirm the separation of church and state on pragmatic grounds, Baptists, as Carter reminded us, affirm it on theological grounds—as that principle which best ensures the freedom of conscience so essential to genuine worship of God. But separating church and state does not remove the belief held by most Americans, even by most Baptists, that the nation—as a civil entity—is still somehow obligated to God, that our nationhood makes little sense unless it is part of a universe ruled by God, that there remains a religious face on the body politic. Stated in another way, religion is not merely private; it is inescapably public too. In his now famous 1967 article, "Civil Religion in America," Robert Bellah acknowledged this, arguing that separation of church and state does not deny the political realm a religious dimension.[5] Within this religious dimension Baptists find their religious liberty founded in the God of the scriptures.

There are those among us who would not accept this characterization. There are those who throw up red flags at the term "civil religion," allowing only the possibility that civil religion must mean either some watered down, lowest-common-denominator religion, or else the exaltation and worship of the nation. Civil religion might mean either of these, but either perspective reflects a limited understanding of what civil religion is at its core. For Baptists, in the strong tradition of religious liberty, civil religion also means that we can and do share with other citizens, whatever their faith, a commitment to the nation and the principles of freedom and democracy upon which it was founded.

An analogy might be of some help here. The apostle Paul takes the time in several of his letters advising Christians regarding meat that has been sacrificed to idols. There is no inherent danger for the Christian in eating such meat, Paul tells us. But if a brother or sister is offended or caused to stumble, the Christian is to abstain; but the concern is for the other, not for the meat. In making these admonitions, Paul presumes that the meat is not spoiled. Of course he would not recommend spoiled meat to anyone, Christian or not! Unfortunately, some regard every instance of civil religion as spoiled meat. This problem, though, is definitional; defining civil religion as either some watered-down, lowest-common-denominator religion, or else the exaltation and worship of the nation, denies the true nature of the religious liberty for which Baptists have shed their blood and given their lives over the centuries.

Not all expressions of civil religion are appropriate for the Christian. Some, we may argue, are not appropriate for anyone. But we cannot throw the baby out with the bath water. In a liberal democracy such as ours, in the increasingly pluralistic society in which we live, we must find some basis on which to share goals and aspirations, ideas and dreams, for our nation. These collective concerns may be described as including a religious dimension; hence, civil religion.

Baptists historically have a total and complete dedication to the separation of church and state that can hardly be matched. As former U.S. Supreme Court chief justice Charles Evans Hughes once expressed it, the commitment to religious freedom and separation of church and state "is the glory of the Baptist heritage, more distinctive than any other characteristic of belief or practice. To this militant leadership all sects and faiths are debtors."[6] And as historian Anson Phelps Stokes wrote almost a half century ago, "No denomination has its roots more firmly planted in the soil of religious freedom and church-state separation than the Baptists."[7] Baptists also realize that our claims to religious liberty that result in the doctrine of separation of church and state are grounded in the identity and character of the God whom we serve. As such, we must acknowledge that not everyone's claims for religious liberty and civil and human rights are so grounded. We would never ask a Hindu or a Buddhist to make similar claims. Nor would we ever demand that an atheist or agnostic admit that the source of our freedom is our being created in the image of God, but neither would we deny such an individual any of the freedoms we enjoy. Equal freedom of conscience for all is the essence of religious liberty.

Our support for these basic human rights and individual liberties doubtless has a religious dimension. Having said that the grounding for such rights and liberties need not be identical for everyone, we must accept that the grounding is in a religious dimension rather than in a particular religion. The civil religion here asserted is not a religion that in any way infringes upon one's particular religion, nor does it call for any relinquishing of loyalty to one's faith or faith community. It means, rather, that among and between faith communities, and those who claim no faith at all, America as a nation has a shared body of beliefs or principles that have a religious quality or dimension to them that inform the way we understand ourselves and how we act as the political entity called the United States of America.

An interesting characteristic of this religious dimension is that it cannot be viewed well from outside or circumscribed for analysis. Ah, but Baptists know this. We know that our faith cannot be explained by someone who does not share it, that our God cannot be described by an atheist. In this light, look again at Jesus' words: "If you continue in my word, you are truly my disciples, and you shall know the truth, and the truth shall make you free" (John 8:31-32).

I do not want merely to explain this civil religion, this religious dimension of the political realm. I want also to show, by reference to this passage, why it is not idolatrous for Christians. It is, in fact, the most "Baptist" way to interpret the curious American way of relating the free church to the limited state. The point is not to justify a particular version of an American civil religion, but rather to show that civil religion is not by definition idolatrous for Christians, nor is it the trivialization of particular religious faiths in favor of a lowest-common-denominator national religion.

This passage from John is one of the best known in the New Testament, especially among those used to support religious liberty. View it in the context of our own day. We are all on a journey, a journey with God, and our journey brings us to the truth. As we journey we can know the truth; in fact, we walk with and are led by the truth. As we all know, also in John's Gospel is the outlandish claim by Jesus that "I am the way, the truth, and the life." The truth we know is Jesus Christ as Savior. The freedom that we know is freedom as disciples of Christ.

More than two hundred years ago a nation was founded that recognized this freedom. This nation was not founded upon the freedom offered by Jesus to his disciples, but upon a promise that the government would not infringe upon the freedom offered in Christ. The government's promise was not simply to Christians to protect their religious freedom, but to all, no matter their god, no matter their faith. The state's commitment as proclaimed in the first sixteen words of the First Amendment ("Congress shall make no law respecting an establishment of religion, or prohibiting the free exercise thereof") was a limit upon the state without reference to a particular religion.

As Paul said in Galatians 5:1, "It is for freedom that Christ has set us free." We find our freedom in Christ. As we continue as his disciples, we know the truth and the truth frees us. Frees us for what? Frees us to live lives that are pleasing to God.

Now this Christian freedom is not dependent upon the First Amendment, a democratic form of government, family values, or anything else, but on Christ. But what a joy it is to live in a land where the freedom that we have in Christ is recognized by the state! Of course a similar freedom is accorded to those of non-Christian faiths. What's more, the First Amendment prohibits government from siding with any particular religious view, which serves as a supporting guarantee that every American's right to the free exercise of religion will be respected. What freedom it is to live in the United States where, for the first time in history, with the ratification of the First Amendment in 1791, the state declared itself prohibited from infringing upon or taking away from the freedoms that can be offered only by religions!

Christians are free in Christ, and, in the United States, our freedom is constitutionally recognized. We are free to exercise our faith as our faith dictates. Our faith cannot be contained within some "private" sphere. Nor does the freedom Christ offers us only have effect in the prayer closet. The United States does not attempt to demand such of its citizens.

One of my favorite cartoons is a Ziggy block, where, standing before a gorgeous sunset, Ziggy utters the simple cheer: "Yeah, God!" When I see a beautiful sunset, I thank God. I imagine a Hindu or a Buddhist or a Muslim has a very similar reaction, yet he or she does not give thanks to the God who was incarnate in Christ and who through the Holy Spirit bears witness with my spirit that I am a child of God. It is the same reaction, but it's a different reaction.

Likewise, I thank God for the freedom that we have in the United States. Without claiming that the nation is a religious nation we can, and should, enjoy and celebrate the freedom that we as a nation have declared for all in the Constitution and Bill of Rights. The enjoying and celebrating of this freedom cannot help but have some religious overtones, a religious dimension. This is proper and appropriate civil religion.

If we are not careful, we will refuse to admit that the religious nature of our lives can never be totally separated from the political nature of our lives. Better said, we are a religious people; even in our politics we are seen to be a religious people. And I say this as a committed separationist!

While I have defined and interpreted "civil religion" different from them, Spivey, Hatfield, and Gaddy are one hundred percent on target with their dire warnings. There **is** a constant danger of idolatry or of watering down our Christian faith! We in the United States stand in constant jeopardy of replacing our thankfulness to God for the freedoms of this nation with a worship **of** the nation. We stand in constant jeopardy of replacing our recognition of God as the source of all authority and acting as though the government ought to act with the authority of God. We stand in constant jeopardy of replacing a reverence for the national heroes who have bled and died for freedom with a sanctifying of national heroes as God's warriors. We stand in constant jeopardy of replacing the particular faiths and particular histories of the peoples of this nation with a perverted story that claims this nation is the fruition of a divine plan for the universe.

Perhaps the problem is that many modern Baptists have forgotten from whence we came. Roger Williams, John Clarke, Obadiah Holmes, Isaac Backus, John Leland, and the rest fought long and hard for religious liberty—not just for themselves, but for everyone. Baptists were in the minority then, but they were a very vocal minority. In standing up for their religious freedom, as a minority, they were also arguing for the religious freedom of others.

Now the tide has turned. No, we Baptists are not a majority of the population, but we are the largest Protestant denomination in the nation. We have access to the halls of power of the federal government, as well as many state governments. Even if we are not the majority we are more a majority than a minority. As such it is important to remember our earlier years when as a minority we spoke loud and clear for liberty. We must be more careful now, to hear the voices of those in minority, but we must forever continue to stand for liberty. If our faith means anything to us, if, as Jude tells us, it is the "once for all delivered to the saints" faith, then we cannot help but see its influence, even in our political lives.

An American civil religion must always be cautious of its place between religion and politics. It can be, but need not be, worship of the nation, which is idolatry. It can be, but need not be, a lowest-common-denominator religion. It is, at the very least, a recognition that our nation stands always under the sovereignty and potential judgment of God. What it is at its best, and what it ought to be, is the overflow of the religious faiths of the citizenry into every aspect of their lives. Baptists have never been good about containing the overflow from their relationship with God. Let us not begin now.[8]

Notes

[1] Jim Spivey, "Separation No Myth: Religious Liberty's Biblical and Theological Bases," *Southwestern Journal of Theology* 36:10-12.

[2] Cited in James Leo Garrett, Jr., " 'Civil Religion': Clarifying the Semantic Problem," *Journal of Church and State* 16 (Spring 1974): 193.

[3] C. Welton Gaddy, "Christian Citizenship 1988," *Report From the Capital* 43 (February 1988): 5.

[4] Cited in Ronald B. Flowers, "President Jimmy Carter, Evangelism, Church-State Relations, and Civil Religion," *Journal of Church and State* 25 (Winter 1983): 121.

[5] Robert Bellah, "Civil Religion in America," *Daedalus* 96 (1967): 1.

[6] Cited in Rufus W. Weaver, ed., *The Road to Freedom of Religion* (Washington DC: Joint Conference committee on Public Relations, 1944) 13.

[7]Anson Phelps Stokes, *Church and State in the United States* (New York: Harper and Brothers, 1950) 3:485.

[8]In the preparation of this sermon, I want to acknowledge with gratitude the research assistance of Steven C. Heyduck, a doctoral fellow at the J. M. Dawson Institute.

Freedom Talk
Conversations of Jesus with Baptists of North America

J. Alfred Smith, Sr.

So if the Son makes you free, you will be free indeed. (John 8:36)

Introduction

Most Americans become misty-eyed when the national anthem is sung. The part that touches Americans most tenderly is the expression "the land of the free and the home of the brave." Good Americans are too close to the pain of the Vietnam War to relish the thoughts of "bombs bursting in the air." It is the closing emphasis of *The Star Spangled Banner* that marries the concepts of bravery and freedom that stirs the emotions so very deeply. The emergence of militia groups across the length and breadth of America, however, motivates us to ask how brave and free we really are.

The Baptist Ministers' Union of Oakland, California, and The East Bay sponsors annually on January 1 an Emancipation Day service that is well attended by the African-American community. I have attended these services for at least ten years. The focus of the preaching by some of the nation's well known orators has been on chattel slavery, emancipation, reconstruction, segregation, and the civil rights movement. Very few preachers, however, have addressed the meaning and quality of freedom for themselves, their children, and grandchildren on the eve of the twentieth century. This blind spot of Baptists is being addressed in the white community by angry white men and by militia groups and in the black community by Minister Louis Farrakhan and Muslims as well as by youthful *gansta rappers* who have never heard of Dr. Martin Luther

King, Jr. Are we Baptists in denial of our own slavery as were the Jews who challenged the liberation ideas of Jesus in John 8:31-38?

A Biblical Parallel

Conflicting definitions of freedom manifested themselves in the dialogue between Jesus and certain of his Jewish followers. Said Jesus, "If you continue in my word, you are truly my disciples; and you will know the truth, and the truth will make you free" (John 8:31).

This statement apparently severely irritated his Jewish disciples. They were so defensive that they became sick unto death with historical amnesia. Had not the children of Abraham, Isaac, and Jacob known the oppressive years of Egyptian, Babylonian, Persian, and Roman captivity and control? Was not monarchy dead in Israel? Why then did they respond to Jesus with words of arrogance, pride, and ethnocentrism? "We are descendants of Abraham and have never been slaves to anyone. What do you mean by saying, 'You will be made free' " (John 8:33-34)?

We are Baptists! We are the children of Roger Williams and Elder Palmer. We *are* free! Baptists in America were born from the womb of freedom. What do you mean Jesus by saying, "You will be made free"? Will Baptists in America be free? Is the question an indictment of who we are in the present, or is it a prophetic word of hope? A correct answer to the question comes only if Baptists can accept the teaching of Jesus: "If you continue in my word, you are truly my disciples; and you will know the truth and the truth will make you free" (John 8:31-32).

"Well," say we Baptists, "Jesus, this is no problem. We are people of The Book. We know your word. We are not a creedal people. We teach that your written word is the rule and guide for our faith and practice."

"Yes," says Jesus. "But does your praxis match your theology? Do you know the truth of your history? What does your history say about you in relationship to slavery and freedom?"

Jesus Talks with Southern Baptists

Jesus: "Are you a slave to your history? Why aren't you my disciples? Why do you use the name Southern? What memories are impregnated in the name Southern Baptists? Are you free because you were slave holders?"

Southern Baptists: "Lord, did you not hear that we apologized to our African-American brothers and sisters for our part in slavery? We know that they have forgiven us because a large number of African-American churches are in our convention and some pastors are graduates of our seminaries?"

Jesus: "Yes, this may be true. But are you supporting mean spirited politicians who give tax breaks to the wealthy while balancing the federal budget on the backs of the poor and elderly? Why are you failing to be an advocate for innocent children whose mothers may be on welfare? Did you not read how Boaz treated the illegal alien from Moab? Did he not only provide her with gleanings, but also the affirmative action of sheaves? 'When she got up to glean, Boaz instructed his young men, "Let her glean even among the standing sheaves, and do not reproach her. You must also pull out some handfuls for her from the bundles, and leave them for her to glean, and do not rebuke her" '(Ruth 2:15-16). Did the social justice mouthpiece of your convention support a supreme court nominee who had an anemic record on racial justice? Are you a slave of culture, and are your struggles for the leadership of your boards and institutions a slavery to control and power much like the takeover of smaller economic entities in the corporate world where mammon is God? Was my ministry in your midst one of takeover and control? Did I not wash the feet of my disciples? No national leader is a messiah. I alone walked on earth without staining my hands with the touch of sin. Such purity and devotion produced my painful death and the ugly scandal of the cross. Could you have not have known that the feet of all of your presidents are made of clay and embraced your own Jimmy Carter and Bill Clinton with redemptive love as did The National Baptists? Are you slaves of legalism? Have you not experienced Amazing Grace?"

Jesus Talks With National Baptists

Jesus: "National Baptists, why are you divided into four national denominations? Do you not sing in your worship services a spiritual that you have named: 'There Is a Balm in Gilead'? Why has it not healed your four national denominations so that my message will attract younger African-American males drawn to the nation of Islam? Did not James Melvin Washington, your premier African-American Baptist historian write about: *Frustrated Fellowship, The Black Baptist Quest for Social*

Power?[1] Will you bequeath to the unborn of the twenty-first century an enduring legacy of denominational tribalism?"

"What have you done with the liberating vision of Martin Luther King, Jr.? Is not your factionalism the Black Baptist scandal of the crucified community that has too long known both the cross of white racism and the cross of self-inflicted Black suffering? If you were one in the reconciling action of the gospel, could you not address the issue of the ultimate liberation of a community of youth who know more about the gospel of rap music than they know about the nonviolent gospel of Martin Luther King, Jr? In slavery you had full employment. Now your young men who comprise six percent of the nation's population constitute fifty percent of the nation's prison population. These young men are the new slaves who work for seventy cents an hour in the prison industries of the land. Those who are unemployed in your inner cities where industries have moved to the third world have the lone option of participating as drug dealers in an ever growing underground economy that makes slaves to narcotic addiction of many young people who are trapped in urban waste lands."

Jesus Talks with American Baptists

Jesus: "American Baptists, where are you? Are you more American than Baptist? Have you given up the Christ of the cross for the Christ of culture? Was not Walter Rauschenbusch one of your prophets? The prophetic preaching of Shailer Mathews, Walter Rauschenbusch, and Harry Emerson Fosdick has been muted so that younger prophetic voices are seldom heard in your biennial meetings. Instead of responding to your own Henry Mitchell's call for the recovery of preaching, sermons are relegated to one of your many simultaneous seminars called pavilions. When a Christian counter culture is needed to challenge the ethics of the Christian Right, you are paralyzed with debates that lead to nowhere on Gay and Lesbian issues that neglect the evangelistic and missionary agenda of the church. Can this greying denomination of older members and aging clergy refocus its energy on its historic legacy of love for God and the world so that Baptists in the North will not resemble the mainline churches of Europe, which now have beautiful buildings for worship but only sparsely filled pews?"

Jesus Speaks to All Baptists

Jesus: "As The Living Lord of history I have spoken to you who are called Baptists about your deficits. All of your conventions have fallen short of my glory. But, I am still the God of grace and glory. There is still time for Baptist denominations in America to conqueror successfully mutual challenges and to resolve unresolved questions."

Prophetic Hope

Let us look to the future with optimism because it takes only a little leaven to make the loaf. It takes only a little seed to grow a healthy plant. God is the God of the living. Our God knows how to make dead bones live. A number of dedicated disciples are members in each of our Baptist denominations. As we continue to share their faith in Jesus, our living Lord, liberation from captivity will come. God will renew the church. Our God is silently liberating and empowering Baptists to proclaim with word and deed the liberation of Christ from the slavery of all moral, social, political, economic, and spiritual evils. Inspiration is ours for the sharing of liberating visions. This inspiration comes from the mothers and fathers of our Baptist legacy.

Though they were slaves, they were free. No chains were upon their minds or their spirits. Like Abraham they looked for a city. Like Joseph in prison in Egypt, they kept the dream alive. Like Paul and Silas, they sang through captivity at midnight. Though captives physically, their spiritual freedom in Christ released their creative imagination to give birth to spirituals such as:

> Done made my vow to the Lord,
> and I never will turn back,
> I will go I shall go,
> to see what the end will be.
> My strength, Good is almost gone,
> I will go,
> I shall go to see what the end will be.
> But you have told me to press on.
> I will go, to see what the end will be.[7]

Such was the testimony of George Liele, a slave preacher, who founded in 1779 the First Negro Baptist Church of Savannah, Georgia. In 1784 he founded the first Negro Baptist Church in Kingston, Jamaica. Such was the testimony of Miss Emma B. Delaney who, by faith, went to Africa in 1902 during the era of segregation and built schools in Liberia and British Central Africa. She rescued young Daniel Malekebu from more than two hundred miles of jungles infested with lions and tigers. She brought him to America and sponsored his education. After graduation from Meharry Medical School in Nashville, Tennessee, in 1917, Dr. Daniel Malekebu married Miss Flora Zeto of the Belgium Congo who had graduated from Spelman College in Atlanta, Georgia. They returned to Africa and supervised medical missions in South East and Central Africa.[3] Our elders lived and proclaimed the Baptist vision of liberty.

Prophetic judgment reveals the downside of our captivity to culture as Baptists. Hence, we speak of slavery. But prophetic hope proclaims the upside of our freedom. Therefore, we speak not of the deficits of our creature like existence as children of dust, but of our possibilities based on the divinity of Christ within us. As Howard Thurman says:

> Did you ever see such a man as God?
> A little more faith in Jesus,
> A preaching the gospel to the poor,
> a little more faith in Jesus.[4]

Jesus identified with the poor, the powerless, and the oppressed of the land. Jesus calls all Baptist bodies into a new freedom "outside the realm of economic wealth, military might, and political power, and inside the world of millions who are being wasted by numerous forms of social, economic and political evils."[5] Our obedience to Christ will liberate us from the prisons of our cultural enslavement. Our obedience to Christ will unite us not in only verbalizing the gospel from pulpits but in living out the ethical and moral demands of the gospel. This man called Jesus took up the cause of the weak and the meek. He challenges Baptists to become advocates for personal transformation and societal justice. Christ calls Baptists to a witness of freedom that liberates persons from the captivity of racism, sexism, and militarism.

Conclusion

Jesus calls us to true freedom. Jesus frees us to experience joy in the midst of pain, hope in the midst of despair, faith in the midst of doubt, strength in the midst of weakness, and life in the midst of death. Jesus calls us to lifestyles of personal sacrifice in a success centered society where church buildings are more important than the needs of the suffering and needy.

"Come, Lord and free us of cultural captivity. May we serve as your slaves in this world with lifestyles of the Living Christ."

Notes

[1] James Melvin Washington, *Frustrated Fellowship: The Black Quest for Social Power* (Macon GA: Mercer University Press, 1986).

[2] Howard Thurman, *The Negro Speaks of Life and Death* (New York: Harper and Row, 1947) 34-35.

[3] Edward A. Freeman, *The Epoch of Negro Baptists and the Foreign Mission Board* (Kansas City: The Central Seminary Press, 1953) 41, 111.

[4] Thurman, *The Negro Speaks*, 38.

[5] Orlando E. Costas, *Christ Outside the Gate* (Maryknoll NY: Orbis Press, 1988) 185.

The Mystery of Iniquity
The Helwys Tradition

Rosalie Beck

> When they had brought them, they had them stand before the council. The high priest questioned them, saying, "We gave you strict orders not to teach in this name, yet here you have filled Jerusalem with your teaching and you are determined to bring this man's blood on us." But Peter and the apostle answered, "We must obey God rather than any human authority. The God of our ancestors raised up Jesus, whom you had killed by hanging him on a tree. God exalted him at his right hand as Leader and Savior that he might give repentance to Israel and forgiveness of sins. And we are witnesses to these things, and so is the Holy Spirit whom God has given to those who obey him." (Acts 5:27-32)

The men had peered from behind doorways. The women had scurried down alleys to avoid being noticed. These people had longed only for no one to tie them to the dead Nazarene, Jesus the Crucified. Suddenly, from Pentecost onward, these same nameless, faceless, and fearful folks came alive with boldness and power, proclaiming what they called the Good News. The same men and women who had avoided official temple or Roman notice now strode courageously into the temple or preached in the marketplace, declaring the resurrection and ascension of Jesus of Nazareth, the one condemned by the Jewish leaders and executed by the Romans.

Christians know this story well. The Holy Spirit empowered the women and men in the upper room and the world changed forever. The specific incident presented in Acts 5:17-32 focuses on the trouble caused by Peter and John as they preached and healed in the temple environs. Jailed at the command of the high priest for their activities, the two men remained in jail only a short time before an angel freed them. In the power of God, they did not flee, as they did when the guards arrested Jesus, but at the command of the angel they returned to the temple to preach and teach about the Risen Lord.

The temple guards located the missing prisoners and brought them before the Sanhedrin, the body of leaders and elders that would decide the fate of the two troublemakers. Commanded by the Sanhedrin not to preach about Jesus, Peter and John stood firm and declared that they must obey God, not humans. If God required them to preach, they would preach, no matter what the Sanhedrin chose to do. Ultimately, Peter and John received a flogging and a command not to preach. They endured the flogging as a sign of God's favor, that they were counted worthy to suffer for the faith, and they ignored the Sanhedrin's command and went their way, proclaiming the Good News of Jesus the Christ.

This passage is rich in vital spiritual principles for twentieth-century Christians. Where to focus is a difficult problem. We could draw lessons on the courage with which we are to identify with Christ publicly, the perseverance we should possess in the face of tribulation, the steadfastness we need in our commitment to God. Principles relating to God's protection of faithful believers, the way God provides power for what the Lord commands, and the need to proclaim the Good News abound in this passage. As attractive and compelling as these themes are, look at a subtext in the story, a principle that is implied rather than overtly presented, a principle by which Baptists have identified themselves from their beginning, but a concept that desperately needs reteaching in our day—the principle of religious liberty.

Throughout their history, Baptists have preached, lived, and died for the belief that each woman and man is responsible to God and accountable to the Lord for their own spiritual relationship. We have taught that every person must choose or reject the gospel and that no external force—family, friends, significant others, governments—has the power to coerce belief in God or acceptance of the Christ as Lord and Savior. *The Baptist Faith and Message* affirms the basic Baptist position on religious liberty:

> A free church in a free state is the Christian ideal, and this implies the right of free and unhindered access to God on the part of all [persons], and the right to form and propagate opinions in the sphere of religion without interference by the civil power.[1]

The Mystery of Iniquity: The Helwys Tradition 145

As basic as the idea of religious liberty is to Baptists, it is a belief and a freedom that must be reaffirmed by each generation. Religious freedom is always one generation from extinction in this, or any, country. But why should we bother to hold this tenet of faith? Are the arguments for religious liberty voiced by our Baptist forefathers and foremothers still valid? The answers to these questions go to the heart of the gospel and to what it means to be a Baptist, and they are exemplified in the response of Peter and John to the command of silence imposed by the Jewish leaders, "We must obey God rather than any human authority" (Acts 5:29).

Henry Ford once said, "History is bunk." Most of us would agree if our only exposure has been to the history teacher who droned on incessantly about the most trivial and boring facts. Thankfully, the writers of the Bible did not agree with Ford's statement. For them, God moves in time and space, and it is through telling and retelling the stories of God's mighty acts that the Truth of the Lord passes from generation to generation. The Psalmist proclaims the need to *remember* in the declaration:

> Walk about Zion, go all around it, count its towers, consider well its ramparts; go through its citadels, that you may tell the next generation that this is God, our God forever and ever. He will be our guide forever (Psalm 42:12-14).

By looking at the lives of our Baptist ancestors, we can glimpse the continuing importance of religious liberty and why so many of them were willing to die to insure that their contemporaries would be free to accept or reject God on God's terms. Our Baptist forebears lived out the words of Peter, and they stood their ground as they proclaimed the right of each human to respond to God or not, as that person chose. Today we remind ourselves that the Lord is "the God who established in the past, sustains in the present, and is in control of the future."

Baptist principles did not spring from thin air. They slowly emerged from the life experiences of people. Just as the Hebrews wrestled with their understanding of God and the early Church struggled to understand the meaning of the Incarnation, early Baptists formulated a concept of religious freedom, religious liberty, freedom of conscience, and soul liberty based on their understanding of who God is and what God requires of the Lord's people.

Central to the belief in the necessity for freedom of conscience is the ancient doctrine of the priesthood of believers. In Exodus 19:4-6, and rehearsed for the Church in 1 Peter 2:9-10, the promise is made that believers will be priests to the world. Being a priest means we have direct access to God and an automatic ministry because of our relationship with God. The word priest comes from the Latin term *pontifex*, which means a *bridge builder*." We are to build bridges from God to the world and from the world to God, to mediate God to the world and the world to God.

As Baptist churches began to develop in the early 1600s, their belief that all Christians are priests before the Lord brought forth an accompanying commitment to religious freedom. In the book of Acts, Peter and John recognized that God must direct their lives, regardless of what civil or religious authorities dictated. In seventeenth-century Europe, Baptists recognized they must be free to pursue their understanding of God's will, but others must have the same freedom to make religious decisions without external coercion. To be a priest meant both the freedom to accept and the freedom to reject the Lord.

The life of Thomas Helwys, an early Baptist leader, exemplifies this Baptist commitment to the principle of religious freedom. He fought for the right of each person to approach or retreat from God without external coercion. He wrote the first plea for complete religious freedom in the English language published in England. He died in prison in 1616, living out his commitment to religious liberty. With his life, Thomas Helwys concretizes the abstract idea of *religious liberty*.

Heir to wealth and privilege, Helwys studied law at Gray's Inn in London, although he was from the country. He married Joan Ashmore in 1595 and settled down as squire at Broxtowe Hall, his ancestral home in Nottinghamshire. He lived well and was a committed member of the church of England until he met and was influenced by a former Anglican priest named John Smyth. Smyth led a group of believers who rejected the Anglican form of worship and many other Church of England practices.

Believing the Church of England impervious to change, they separated from the church and organized in small groups that met secretly to study scripture. These so-called Separatists were considered criminals because they refused to support the state church. King James I hounded the Separatists because he saw them as a threat to his power, and the group led by Smyth made plans to move to Holland where they could worship openly, without governmental reprisal. Helwys, a businessman with shipping interests, paid for the relocation and provided the ships to carry the congregation to Holland and safety.

In July 1607, with relocation preparations underway, Helwys left home to finalize the details. Joan and the children planned to join him before the sailing date, but disaster struck. Before Joan could bundle the children away from Broxtowe Hall, soldiers arrived with a warrant for Helwys's arrest issued by James I. Not finding him on the grounds, the soldiers imprisoned Joan at York Castle and seized the Hall. The children were parceled among relatives, and James gave the Hall to one of his court favorites. Joan remained in prison until the officials realized Helwys, who had sailed with the other Separatists, would not return to Nottinghamshire.

We can only imagine the trauma the couple endured, separated from one another and their children, wrestling with whether or not to give up their new understanding of Christianity in order to resume their lives. They believed they were right and the state and the Church of England were wrong in the demands for religious conformity they made on people's consciences and lives. Both Joan and Thomas Helwys suffered for that belief.

As Joan suffered imprisonment, the Separatists sailed safely to Amsterdam, Holland. Through continued Bible study, prayer, and discussions with believers from other denominations, the Separatists accepted adult believer's baptism. Baptism, they contended, was for persons who knew what they were accepting and proclaiming through the act. The Smyth-Helwys group also accepted the concept of a voluntary and free church, one not tied to the government. For them, the church was a gathered community of people banded together voluntarily. It has an identity distinctly separate from the state. The church does not rely on that state in any way for its existence.

This beginning Baptist consciousness flowered into confessions of faith and acceptance of the name Baptist. In 1612, Helwys led a group back to England, because he "came to the conclusion that it was his duty to return and bear witness to the truth."[2] These Baptist men and women knew they might be called upon to "lay down their lives in their own country for Christ and his truth,"[3] and they willingly accepted that challenge as they settled in Spitalsfield, outside London, and began the first Baptist church on English soil.

Joined by his wife and children, Helwys became the acknowledged leader of the group. When government persecution against dissenters from the Church of England began, Helwys wrote the first plea for complete religious freedom. He dedicated "The Mystery of Iniquity" to James I, because the king was the one person who could alter the laws of the land in favor of religious dissenters. In this tract, Helwys reasoned that people's religion is "betwixt God and themselves; the King shall not answer for it."[4] Arguing that people of different religions, like the Muslim Turks and the Jews, must have religious freedom also, Helwys affirmed that a person's relationship with God is not dependent on any human, and "it apperteynes not to the earthly power to punish them in the least measure."[5]

Helwys, and the other Baptists, held the conviction that each person is responsible to God for his or her own relationship, but also that each person has a ministry under Christ. Each believer, Baptists argued, is a priest. If Christians were to be priests before the Lord, they must have the freedom to mediate their faith to the world. Without this freedom, they could not fulfill God's will. In "The Mystery of Iniquity" Helwys tried to persuade the king that it was in the best interest of the state and Christ's church to extend religious freedom to all, to coerce the consciences of no one, and to allow God's people to become true priests of the Good News.

Helwys argued that true Christianity does not need the help of the state to maintain attendance or gain adherents. True religion calls to unbelievers and draws them to God. He understood that when errors of belief arise they can be dealt with through discussion, prayer, and Bible study. The Bible is the Word of God, a Living Sword, and the scripture needs no earthly help to bring to God. Coercion for religious purposes insults God because it implies the Lord cannot accomplish the divine purpose with the chosen tools of the Bible and the Holy Spirit.

Helwys insisted that trying to rectify error with force never works. People must be persuaded by love, the Word of God, and the Holy Spirit. The state cannot make people conform in their hearts, and the attempt creates hatred, malice, and evil. Only with free and public discourse, Bible study and prayer, can religious error be corrected. And these actions can only take place in a society where religious freedom belongs to each person.

King James I ordered the arrest of Thomas Helwys as a religious dissenter, and Helwys died in prison in 1616. He chose to return to

England to call his fellow-citizens to the light of Christ that he saw. He returned knowing he might die. Helwys chose to face persecution, to suffer the separation and loneliness of prison, and finally to pay the ultimate price for freedom—to die for his faith. He died because he believed in doctrines different from those of the established church. He died, specifically, for writing and publishing a tract pleading for religious freedom as a basic human right. He suffered because he recognized, that while the state may coerce attendance at church and the following of the church's practices, the heart cannot be coerced into believing in or worshiping the Lord. The stand Helwys took, and which we are challenged to accept today, cannot be undertaken lightly, without thought.

Whether or not we choose to support the Baptist position on religious freedom must be carefully considered. Helwys weighed the possible outcome against the importance of his proclamations and writings. He knew what he believed because it meant life or death to him, and he chose to be true to his beliefs, that faith cannot be coerced, that the calling to be a priest cannot be fulfilled except with personal religious freedom. Can we affirm those doctrines as part of our modern Baptist selves? Can we stand with Peter and John in the temple and proclaim our spiritual integrity, our refusal to submit to human limitations when faced with the command of God to go beyond those limits?

Helwys died for his faith. Peter and John suffered a flogging for theirs. As the Acts narrative continues, Gamaliel, the great Jewish teacher and rabbi, advised the Sanhedrin to react less harshly to the followers of Christ. He warned that if these men and women truly represented God, their movement would not be affected by the great council's decisions. And, if the movement came from the Lord, the religious leaders would not want to be found persecuting God's followers. Wise words! Coercion does not change hearts. Only God can do that.

In our day when more and more political rhetoric assume religious overtones, Baptists need to be particularly clear in their understanding of religious freedom. They need to be willing to affirm it, even when they dislike the teachings of a person who wants to exercise this basic human right. Trusting God enough to support complete religious freedom is difficult, but it is at the center of the Baptist tradition. Let us affirm with Thomas Helwys that "it apperteynes not to the earthly power to punish [unbelief] in the least measure," and with Peter and John, "We must obey God rather than human authority." Like generations of Baptists before, and hopefully, after us, let us affirm this great mystery of God's love:

that the Lord gives us the freedom to say "no" just as the Lord grants us the power to say "yes" and become the children of God.

Notes

[1] *The Baptist Faith and Message* (Nashville: The Sunday School Board of the Southern Baptist Convention, 1963) 19. This is a confession of faith adopted by the Southern Baptist Convention, 9 May 1963.

[2] William T. Whitley, *Thomas Helwys of Gray's Inn and Broxtowe Hall, Nottingham* (London: The Kingsgate Press, n.d.) 13.

[3] Ibid.

[4] As cited in Leon McBeth, ed., *A Sourcebook for Baptist Heritage* (Nashville: Broadman Press, 1990) 72.

[5] Ibid.

A Visit from John Clarke

Thomas R. McKibbens

For freedom Christ has set us free. Stand firm, therefore, and do not submit again to a yoke of slavery. (Galatians 5:1)

For you were called to freedom, brothers and sisters; only do not use your freedom as an opportunity for self-indulgence, but through love become slaves to one another. For the whole law is summed up in a single commandment. "You shall love your neighbor as yourself." If, however, you bite and devour one another, take care that you are not consumed by one another.

Live by the Spirit, I say, and do not gratify the desires of the flesh. For what the flesh desires is opposed to the Spirit, and what the Spirit desires is opposed to the flesh; for these are opposed to each other, to prevent you from doing what you want. But if you are led by the Spirit, you are not subject to the law. Now the works of the flesh are obvious: fornication, impurity, licentiousness, idolatry, sorcery, enmities, strife, jealousy, anger, quarrels, dissensions, factions, envy, drunkenness, carousing, and things like these. I am warning you, as I warned you before: those who do such things will not inherit the kingdom of God.

By contrast, the fruit of the Spirit is love, joy, peace, patience, kindness, generosity, faithfulness, gentleness, and self-control. There is no law against such things. And those who belong to Christ Jesus have crucified the flesh with its passions and desires. If we live by the Spirit, let us also be guided by the Spirit. Let us not become conceited, competing against one another, envying one another . (Galatians 5:13–25)

Pardon me for seeming a bit nervous. The last time I preached in Massachusetts I was interrupted in the middle of my sermon and taken off to prison. By the way, do you folk not need anyone watching out for the magistrates? Well, I will tell you more about that experience later, but as most of you do not know me, let me introduce myself.

A Bit about My Background

It was a cold November day in 1637 when my ship arrived here from England. I was in my twenty-ninth year of life, newly married to Elizabeth, and we were reaching out to a new world. My friends in England had told me that I had much to offer such a place as this. Physically I was strong and healthy: more than six feet tall, enthusiastic, a natural leader. And I was well educated: I had received a master of arts degree from the University of Leyden in Holland, and had spent several years working as a physician in London. My academic work at the University of Leyden had prepared me for three professions: medicine, law, and the ministry.

I was fluent in Latin, Greek, and Hebrew, and I had already published an analytical concordance of the Bible for the use of God's ministers. You can find a copy of it still in the Harvard College library. The title may throw you: *"Holy Oyle for the Lampes of the Sanctuarie; or Scripture Phrases Alphabetically Disposed for the Use and Benefit of such as desire to speak the Language of Canaan, more especially the sonnes of the Prophets who would attain elegance and sublimitie of expression."*

The truth is that I was one of the most educated men in all of New England. Does that sound strange to you? You must remember that in the year 1637, the city of Boston had only been in existence for seven years. The city that greeted Elizabeth and me when we walked down that gangplank had only 1,000 inhabitants! What a change hath God wrought since those days!

We thought Boston would be a wonderful and exciting place to begin our married life. How wrong we were! Boston was embroiled in a bitter theological controversy. You must understand that all citizens were required to attend church, and the authority of the clergy was enormous.

No sooner had we set foot on dry land than we heard of the furor over a woman named Anne Hutchinson, who had the gall to question the sermons of John Wilson, the pastor of the church in Boston. Not only did she raise questions about his sermons, she held weekly meetings in her home to discuss his sermon from the previous Sunday. The Hutchinson home was located just across the street from the home of Governor John Winthrop, an ardent supporter of the pastor! So every Wednesday night the governor would see two hundred men and women filing into the Hutchinson house to listen to this woman evaluate the pastor's Sunday sermon!

Three months before we arrived in Boston, the clergy had met and charged Anne Hutchinson with twenty-nine heresies. We arrived in Boston the very month she and her family were banished from Boston.

To be blunt about it, I was sympathetic with her. I knew deep down that the Puritans did not come to America because they wanted true religious freedom; rather they came to America because they wanted to set up religion in this new country the way they thought religion should be conducted. Now they were banishing Anne Hutchinson because she questioned their authority!

Well, I stood with her! I had become a Baptist in Holland, and I had experienced the sweet taste of religious freedom there. I was not about to go back to religious slavery—to the Puritan clergy or to anyone else! Some twenty of us stood shoulder to shoulder with her against the Puritan authorities. The magistrates confiscated our property and disarmed us. We realized that the only thing left for us was to find someplace else to settle. The others turned to me as their natural leader.

A Whipping I'll Never Forget

But where could we and where would we settle? We thought of turning north to the town of Exeter, New Hampshire. Our friend John Wheelwright had founded that town the year before, after being banished by the same Puritan divines. But instead, we decided to go south, perhaps to Long Island. On the way we stopped at Providence Plantations to visit with Roger Williams, who received us warmly. He suggested that we purchase the island of Aquidneck from the Indians. This we promptly did, and then we renamed it Rhode Island. We established the towns of Newport and Portsmouth.

Thus began my long friendship with Roger Williams. But I must tell you that although we shared a passionate belief in freedom of religion, we were opposites in almost every other way. Roger was volatile. He could never make up his mind what he really believed. Sometimes I think that he knew more about what he was against than what he was for! John Quincy Adams later described Roger as "conscientiously contentious"! I suppose he was right!

Roger founded the Baptist church in Providence in 1638, the very year we visited with him. But at most he remained a Baptist three or four months. Soon he rejected his Baptist views, saying that while the Baptists were close, there had to be something even better. So he spent the rest of his life as a self-styled "Seeker"; he was always seeking for the truth.

On the other hand, I was a more settled person. In 1644 I became the first pastor of the Baptist church in Newport, Rhode Island, and I was content to call myself a Baptist for the rest of my natural life, until 1676.

But Roger Williams and I stood side by side on this one thing: we both wanted Rhode Island to be a place of complete religious freedom. We would welcome people of all religions or no religion with equal standing. We became the first colony to accept Jews; the first Jewish synagogue in America was built just down the street from the Baptist church I served. We welcomed Quakers, and the oldest Quaker meeting house in America is in Newport. We became the first colony to give people freedom of conscience in religious matters. And it worked!

Of course, the members of Parliament back in London had a hard time believing it would work. So my fellow citizens sent Roger Williams and me back to London to convince them. This is where my legal training came in handy. I wrote the charter of Rhode Island, signed by King Charles II in 1663. It was that charter that contained the statement: "to hold forth a lively experiment." And it was a lively experiment to have freedom of religion! I was rather proud of that charter, because it served the needs of the people of Rhode Island for one hundred and seventy years. I was pleased to see that Thomas Jefferson used it as one of the sources on which he based the Declaration of Independence.

Back in Newport, my medical training also came in handy. The church could not support me adequately, so as a physician my services were in great demand.

But more than anything else, I was a minister of the gospel. We gathered a wonderful congregation of Baptists in Newport. My two deacons and I were especially close. Their names were Obadiah Holmes and John Crandall. In 1651, I received a letter from an old friend, William Witter. Mr. Witter had grown old and gone blind. He was a Baptist, and he wrote to ask me if I would come to see him and administer communion for the last time. Of course, I could not refuse.

The problem was that Mr. Witter lived in Lynn, Massachusetts, and it was against the law for Baptists to hold a worship service in Massachusetts. So I talked it over with my deacons. "Obadiah and John," I said, "will you go with me?" Of course they agreed. On 19 August 1651, the three of us rode quietly into Lynn. We were well aware of the danger, but we would conduct a quiet communion service and then leave. But there were other Baptists in the area who had heard of our visit. When we arrived, we discovered a rather large crowd who wanted to hear the gospel preached. What was I to do?

We gathered in Mr. Witter's living room for the worship service. In the middle of my sermon, we heard the magistrates coming. They rudely interrupted my discourse and arrested us. We were taken to Boston and thrown into prison. At our trial we were sentenced to pay stiff fines or else receive thirty lashes. For some reason, John Crandall was released on the promise that he would return to a later session of the court. But Obadiah Holmes and I refused to pay our fines. Our consciences would not allow us to do so.

On the day we were taken to the whipping posts, Obadiah seemed more calm than I. It was hard to believe that I was about to have my back torn to shreds because I preached the gospel. When I was tied to the post and was ready for the lash, I received a great surprise. I was told by the magistrate that someone had paid my fine. "Who was it?" I asked. "You'll never know," said the magistrate, "but he is someone who said that he was unwilling to witness a scholar, a gentleman, and a reverend divine in such a situation," he said. So I was freed, and I watched in agony as my friend and deacon Obadiah Holmes received thirty lashes.

As he was being whipped, he spoke to the people. He said, "Though my flesh should fail, and my spirit should fail, yet God would not fail." And as his back was cut to ribbons, something strange happened. Obadiah began to pray, not for himself, but for those who condemned him and punished him. He prayed that God would not lay this sin to their charge, and it seemed that he hardly felt the lash! At the end of that gruesome punishment, he was untied and fell to the ground. He looked up, and said to the man who had administered the whip: "You have struck me as with roses."

Conclusion

I conclude with this story to remind you of the text we read today: "For freedom Christ has set us free. Stand firm, and do not submit again to a yoke of slavery." I have joined you today to remind you of the high price people have paid for that freedom. No one, government or clergy, has power over your conscience in religious matters.

I am here to remind you of your heritage as Christians and as Baptists. I understand that you now celebrate the Declaration of Independence every July Fourth in this great country. I hope that as you celebrate this historic moment in the future that you will remember me and my deacons, and the price we paid for holding a worship service in Lynn. And remember that the struggle for freedom of conscience is constant. It is something about which you can never grow passive.

I am pleased to say that one of my direct descendants became one of the greatest presidents this country ever had and carried on this legacy of freedom. His name is Abraham Lincoln. He was a direct blood descendant; but you, my Baptist friends, are my spiritual descendants. I urge you to carry on the legacy of freedom. Liberty is such a sweet word. Let it sound across the land!

The Love of God and the Worth of Immortal Souls
A Dramatic Monologue Sermon on John Leland

R. Quinn Pugh

[*John Leland (1754–1841) is one of the truly great Baptist advocates of religious liberty to ever live. A native of New England, he spent fourteen years in Virginia, working in both places on behalf of the rights of conscience. While there is no record that John Leland spoke before the 1791 meeting of the General Committee of the Baptists of Virginia, it is not unreasonable to suggest that on this occasion he might have seized one last opportunity to reflect on the struggle for the rights of conscience and the gains for religious liberty in the new federal constitution. This struggle had not been his alone; rather it had been the urgent, often wrenching concern of the General Committee, if not of every Baptist in Virginia. Leland had again and again been their chosen spokesperson. Many portions of this dramatic monologue sermon are the words of John Leland, appropriately set apart by quotation marks and identified by their source. Though these quotations are brought together from various writings of Leland, penned at different times in his life, every attempt has been made to present the unwavering consistency of his passion for religious liberty throughout his fourteen-year sojourn in Virginia.*

The effectiveness of the dramatic monologue sermon is in the preacher's ability and willingness to embody in mind and spirit the character being portrayed. A clear sense of the historical setting (time, place, occasion, atmosphere) is essential in such a portrayal. In this sermon, the setting is the 1791 gathering of the General Committee of Virginia Baptists immediately prior to John Leland's return to his native New England. Leland is speaking to his beloved Virginia Baptists, following a near decade and one half of ministry with an intense involvement in pleading the cause of religious liberty, the implications of which were not merely local, but essentially, national. To interpret Leland, one must not fail to observe that his actions in behalf of the rights of conscience are firmly rooted in his theological understanding of "the love of God, and the worth of immortal souls." It is no surprise that John Leland continues to emerge as a major player in the "American experiment" of religious freedom.]

Thank you, my brother Samuel Harris. You honor me by this unexpected call to stand here today. With due respect for you, Mr. Moderator, and for the delegates present from seven associations, I accept your gracious gesture on this eve of my departure for New England. If my mind serves me well, this is the eighth meeting of the General Committee, representing the Society of Baptists in Virginia.

How very commodious is this meeting house of the Nuckol's congregation situated in goodly Goochland County! It is pleasant to acknowledge the distinguished guests from Georgia who are with us, the Reverend Silas Mercer and the Reverend Jeremiah Walker, whom we shall hear in this meeting respecting their differing Baptist views on the subject of Calvinism. Mr. Moderator, I join you in extending to them the fullsome welcome of their Baptist brethren in Virginia. To digress momentarily, I mention that accompanying Reverend Mercer on his preaching tour of Virginia is his strikingly able young minister-son, the Reverend Jesse Mercer, whom I predict will, without question, show himself to be a great leader among Baptists in the years to come.[1]

So, on this fourteenth day of May, in the year of our Lord 1791, I shall offer a text of benediction, coming from the pen of the Apostle Paul as he prayed for the Philippians: "And the peace of God which passeth all understanding shall keep your hearts and minds through Christ Jesus" (4:7). It is, need I remind you?, that by His grace and through the freedom of your consciences that you know "the peace of God." The apostle's prayer is my prayer today in behalf of this General Committee, and my prayer for the unseen days ahead; for you "are not strangers, my dear brethren and children, to the differences of opinions now subsisting among the Baptists of Virginia."[2]

Therefore, in the spirit of this benediction, allow me to recall the generous benefits of God's sovereign grace among us over these fourteen years of our endeavors together. Indeed, I perceived on my first visit to Virginia in 1775 that this was an "advantageous field for labor."[3] Upon returning to Massachusetts, after eight months in this lovely land, God granted me the blessing of my wife, Sally Devine Leland. Newly wedded, we returned to Virginia in the Fall of 1776.

From first in Mount Poney in Culpepper, where "I was too young and roving" to be a "blessing to the people," I removed to Orange where for the past thirteen years, my family and I have lived and labored. "I have preached about three thousand sermons since I came to Virginia; all of which have been too flat, and many of them so cold, that the sentences would freeze within my lips; and yet many times when I have attempted to instruct and comfort others, I have found the same blessings for myself."[4]

"The love of God, and the worth of immortal souls, has stimulated my heart and borne me under all the pressures of mobs, tumults, reproaches, and contentions; and having obtained help of God, I remain until this day."[5] With me, you recall that from October 1787 until March of 1789, there was a "continual fall of heavenly rain." It was during these sixteen months that I was privileged to baptize four hundred persons; and through the extent of my stay in Virginia, I have "baptized precisely seven hundred persons" and leave behind "two churches gathered under this ministry."[6] Nor shall I forget these years of ministry. Once when preaching in Louisa, alas, "something seemed to descend on the people ... the next day there were five to be baptized. The day was cold. While Mr. Bowles was preaching to the people, I composed this hymn," several verses of which I quote for you this day:

> Christians, if your hearts be warm,
> Ice and snow can do no harm;
> If by Jesus you are prized,
> Rise, believe and be baptized.

> Jesus drank the gall for you,
> Bore the curse for sinners due;
> Children, prove your love to him.
> Never fear the frozen stream.
>
> Never shun the Savior's cross,
> All in earth is worthless dross;
> If the Savior's love you feel,
> Let the world behold your zeal.[7]

"The union that has taken place among the Baptists in Virginia has been very pleasant to me, and a continuation of the same, is an object that engrosses my desire. For this desirable end, I have been willing to sacrifice a number of little peculiarities, and think myself a gainer in the bargain."[8] You are sensible to those differences that continue to be expressed among us, too often with rancor, whether from those "pleading for predestination, and others for universal provision. He cannot be wrong, whose life and heart are right. He cannot walk amiss who walks in love. I have generally observed that when religion is lively among the people, no alienation of affection arises from differences of judgment. I conclude that the eternal purpose of God and the freedom of the human will, are both truths; and it is a matter of fact, that the preaching that has been most blessed of God, and most profitable to man, is the doctrine of sovereign grace in the salvation of souls, mixed with a little of which is called Arminianism."[9] May it be that "the names Regular and Separate be buried in oblivion. It is plain that all party spirit is now laid aside, and that it was a union of heart as well as parties."[10]

Now, I turn with you, my fellow delegates, to recount the blessings of Divine Peace with which our Sovereign Lord has kept our hearts and minds as we strove together in consideration of "all the political grievances of the whole Baptist Society in Virginia." Among these urgent matters were "the law for the solemnization of marriages and the vestry law . . . the law for a general assessment and that for the incorporation of religious societies."[11]

Together, we heartily acknowledge our brother Reuben Ford, clerk of this Body from our first meeting, who has served us well in the earliest presentations on our behalf before the honorable General Assembly. The resolution of 1785 stated firmly our Baptist position respecting "the engrossed bill for a general assessment for the support of teachers of the Christian religion," such bill it was "believed to be repugnant to the spirit of the gospel . . . no human laws ought to be established for this purpose; but that every person ought to be left entirely free in respect to matters of religion; that the holy Author of our religion needs no such compulsive measures for the promotion of His cause; that the gospel wants not the feeble arm of man for its support; that it has made, and will again through divine power, make its way against all opposition; and that should the Legislature assume the right of taxing the people for the support of the gospel, it will be destructive to religious liberty."[12]

When the bill for assessment came before the General Assembly, it did not pass, but on the contrary, an act passed explaining the nature of religious liberty. This law was drawn by the venerable Thomas Jefferson. The opposition made to the bill of assessment by the Baptists, provided for its inhibition before the Assembly. May it ever be that those who hold as precious the freedom of conscience, oppose, as individuals, such tyrannies as legislate against religious choice and practice. As individuals, we of the Baptist society stood in opposition; individuals from the Presbyterians and others joined us, though their clergy grew timid in the fray.

You of this General Committee of the Baptist Society in Virginia appointed me with the honored responsibility, alongside others, of waiting on the General Assembly for the presentation of a memorial concerning the distribution of lands previously assigned to an established religious Society. It was about this time that I encountered an Episcopal clergyman who heard me at one of my meetings denounce the state support of the ministry of any church. Confronting me, he said, "The minister should get tax support so he will not have such a hard time preparing his sermons." To this, my reply was, "I am able to expound the scriptures without any special preparation." Not content with my response, this state supported minister thought to expose me with his challenge, "Let's see if you can. What, for instance, would you do with Numbers 22:21, 'And Balaam . . . saddled his ass'? I immediately gave the setting of this passage and proceeded to make application, declaring, "First, Balaam, as a false prophet, represents a state-hired clergy; second, the saddle represents the enormous tax burden of their salaries; third, the dumb ass represents the people who bear such a burden. "Needless to say, I heard no more from the likes of him as the story of this encounter has spread throughout the region.[13]

Of greater concern to the General Committee in 1788, as you so well recall, was "whether the new Federal Constitution, which had now lately made its appearance in public, made sufficient provisions for the secure enjoyment of religious liberty; on which, it was agreed unanimously that, in the opinion of the General Committee, it did not."[14] This issue exercised my mind and spirit with the greatest of agitation. Mr. Madison had, in his Memorial and Remonstrance to the General Assembly, convincingly laid down the case for religious liberty, a case that prevailed in the state of Virginia; but no such provision was made by the Constitutional Convention of the new United States. What was more troubling, Mr. Madison was the primary architect of the document approved and sent forth by this Convention. It was, when he stood before the legislative body of Virginia, as it is now, before the United States, a matter of the rights of conscience; and the rights of conscience are inalienable. "Conscience will ever judge right when it is rightly informed, and speak the truth when it understands it. . . . Does a man, upon entering into social compact, surrender his conscience to that society, to be controlled by the laws thereof; or can he, in justice, assist in making laws to bind his children's consciences before they are born? I judge not." And so judged the delegates of the Baptist Society to the General Committee in their objection to the new Federal Constitution.[15]

Let it be affirmed today among us, and reaffirmed by generations to come that "every man must give an account of himself to God in a way that he can reconcile to his conscience. If no government can answer for individuals on the day of judgment, then let men be free. But supposing it was right for a man to bind his conscience, yet surely it is very iniquitous to bind the consciences of his children—to make fetters for them before they are born, is very cruel. And yet such has been the conduct of men in almost all ages, that their children have been bound to believe and worship as their fathers did, or suffer shame, loss, and sometimes life, and at best to be called dissenters, because of their dissent from that which they never joined voluntarily. Religion is a matter between God and individuals: the religious opinions of men not being the object of civil government, nor in any way under its control."[16] From Constantine, did not religion receive a deadly wound by being fostered in the arms of civil power and regulated by law? It was the absence of these guarantees of the rights of conscience in the new federal constitution that inflamed the opposition of the General Committee.

Having agreed to stand for election in Orange County as a delegate to the Virginia ratifying convention, I wrote in full my specific objections to this document of Constitution, stating "There is no Bill of Rights; whenever a number of men enter into a state of Society, a number of individual rights must be given up to Society, but there should be a memorial to those not surrendered, otherwise, every natural and domestic right becomes alienable, which raises tyranny at once; and this is necessary in one form of Government as in another. . . . What is clearest of all—religious liberty is not sufficiently secured, no religious test is required to fill any office under the United States, but if a majority of Congress with the president favor one system more than another, they may oblige all to pay to the support of this system as much as they please, and if oppression does not ensue, it will be owing to the mildness of administration and not to any constitutional defense, and if the manners of people are so far corrupted, that they cannot live by republican principles, it is very dangerous leaving religious liberty at their mercy."[17]

In every way, the great majority of our Baptist Society, having suffered the abuses of religious oppression, agreed with the views which I set forth, though we earnestly considered the undesirable contrary results of having no instrument of government to bind together the several states North and South should the constitution fail ratification.

By a series of events and sundry communications, upon his return to Virginia, and particularly upon the insistence of our Baptist brother, Captain Joseph Spencer, who once himself was imprisoned for his faith, Mr. Madison determined to go considerably out of his way to meet with me on the Fredricksburg Road before reaching Orange. It had become a matter of pressing evidence that because of our Baptist opposition to the absence of a Bill of Rights, Virginia would not ratify the federal constitution to which he had so diligently given his efforts.

The day came for our meeting. Only the Eternal Creator recorded the extent of our intense arguments, and only the solemn oaks were witnesses to our deliberate determinations. With the highest respect for each other and with the utmost confidence in the honesty of our separate positions, we struggled for half a day to determine how liberty of conscience might be secured for all citizens of the United States. On the principle of religious liberty we agreed; on the procedure for securing that principle we debated at length until it was settled with Mr. Madison's pledge that if elected as the Orange delegate to the ratifying convention, he would introduce an amendment to the constitution in the first Congress guaranteeing a Bill of Rights. His word was sufficient for me.

When we gathered to address the constituency at the picnic grounds in Orange, Mr. Madison spoke logically and convincingly for two hours as he stood on a hogshead of tobacco from which he might be seen and heard by all the people. Following his clear and unvarnished presentation, I stood before the large gathering, all of whom I knew and held with genuine respect. Instead of countering the remarks of Mr. Madison, I heartily withdrew my candidacy in support of our esteemed neighbor and trusted friend of religious liberty upon his assurance that little time would pass in the first congress before "the most satisfactory provision for essential rights, particularly of conscience in the fullest latitude" would be put forward.[19]

You, my brothers and children, know the outcome of these efforts: with the encouragement of Mr. Jefferson, though still in Paris, the unfailing support of General Washington, our new president, and the diligence of Mr. Madison, we now have an amendment to the federal constitution, a Bill of Rights that protects our liberty in matters of religion. As it so stands with the unprecedented amendment, the federal constitution is without compare in all the governments of the world.

Praying that the peace of God will keep our hearts and minds, it is thus becoming of us to raise together voices of thanksgiving to Him who is the Author of our Freedom. And heeding the counsel of the Apostle Paul, let us "stand fast therefore in the liberty wherewith Christ has made us free" (Galatians 5:1). Having worked ceaselessly to secure the rights given by God to all humankind, so we must tirelessly engage our efforts to maintain the freedom of conscience now protected by the Constitution. Those forces so long dominant in the governments of the earth, whether of the state or of religious societies, are yet alive to rescind the gains of freedom and to tyrannize the inalienable rights of conscience.

"My children, I am afraid that after my departure, you will forget the weak advise that I have given you; and what is infinitely more the instruction of that gracious Redeemer who bought you with his blood. Wherefore watch and remember that for the space of fourteen years, I ceased not to warn you night and day, and taught you publicly, and from house to house. And now, behold, I go, with submission to Providence, to New England, not knowing what things will befall me there. Perhaps the faithless seas may be my tomb, or I may live to experience more severe trials then ever I have sustained."[19] Nevertheless, I go; and as I go, I commend you to the "peace of God." Amen

Notes

[1] Robert B. Semple, *Rise and Progress of the Baptists in Virginia* (1810; ed. G. W. Beale, reissued in Richmond, 1894) 106.

[2] L. F. Greene, ed. *The Writings of the Late Elder John Leland* (New York: Printed by G. W. Wood, 1845) 177.

[3] William B. Sprague, *Annals of the American Pulpit* (New York: Robert Caster and Brothers, 1865) 6:175.

[4] Greene, *Writings*, 178.

[5] Ibid.

[6] David Douglas Burhans, "A Study and Evaluation of John Leland's Contribution to American Religious Liberty" (Th.M. thesis, The Southern Baptist Theological Seminary, 1966) 25.

[7] Greene, *Writings*, 28.

[8] Ibid., 177. The union among Baptists to which Leland refers is the union between Regular Baptists and Separate Baptists. Regulars were Calvinistic in theology; Separates were less so, often referred to as Arminians.

[9] Ibid.

[10] Semple, *Rise and Progress*, 101.

[11] Ibid., 95.

[12] Ibid., 96-97.

[13] Joseph Martin Dawson, *Baptists and the American Republic* (Nashville: Broadman Press, 1956) 97.

[14] Semple, *Rise and Progress*, 102.

[15] Greene, *Writings*, 181.

[16] Ibid.

[17] Burhans, "A Study and Evaluation," 41-42.

[18] Irving Brant, *James Madison, Father of the Constitution* (New York: Bobbs-Merrill, 1950) 240.

[19] Greene, *Writings*, 172.

Biographical Data

Rosalie Beck is professor of religion at Baylor University in Waco, Texas.

Michael Bledsoe is pastor of the Riverside Baptist Church in Washington DC.

Carolyn DeArmond Blevins is associate professor of religion at Carson-Newman College in Jefferson City, Tennessee.

William H. Brackney is principal of McMaster Divinity College and professor of historical theology in Hamilton, Ontario, Canada.

Derek H. Davis is director of the J. M. Dawson Institute of Church-State Studies at Baylor University and editor of the *Journal of Church and State*.

James M. Dunn is executive director of the Baptist Joint Committee on Public Affairs in Washington DC.

Stan Hastey is executive director of The Alliance of Baptists in Washington DC and a former staff member of the Baptist Joint Committee on Public Affairs in Washington.

Roger Hayden is general superintendent of the Western Area of The Baptist Union of Great Britain.

Thomas R. McKibbens, Jr., is pastor of the First Baptist Church in Newton Center, Massachusetts.

E. Y. Mullins, who died in 1928, was president of The Southern Baptist Theological Seminary from 1899–1928; he also served as president of the Southern Baptist Convention and the Baptist World Alliance.

R. Quinn Pugh is retired executive director-treasurer of the Baptist convention of New York.

Walter B. Shurden is editor of the series *Proclaiming the Baptist Vision* and Callaway Professor and chair of The Roberts Department of Christianity at Mercer University in Macon, Georgia.

J. Alfred Smith, Sr. is senior pastor of the Allen Temple Baptist Church in Oakland, California.

George W. Truett, who died in 1944, was pastor of First Baptist Church of Dallas, Texas, for forty-seven years; he also served as president of both the Southern Baptist Convention and the Baptist World Alliance.

Brent Walker is the general counsel for the Baptist Joint Committee on Public Affairs in Washington DC.